Creating Access

Language and Academic Programs
for Secondary School Newcomers

Printed in the United States of America
10 9 8 7 6 5 4 3 2 1

Professional Practice Series 3

Editorial/production supervision: Jeanne Rennie
Copyediting: Elizabeth Peterson and Jeanne Rennie
Design and cover: SAGARTdesign

ISBN 1-887744-87-8

Prepared for publication by the ERIC Clearinghouse on Languages and Linguistics. Published by the Center for Applied Linguistics and by Delta Systems Co., Inc.

Funding for the writing of this publication and for the research described herein was provided by the Center for Research on Education, Diversity & Excellence through the following cooperative agreement:

U.S. Department of Education
Institute of Education Sciences
Cooperative Agreement No. R306A60001-96

Funding for the editing and production of the book was provided by the ERIC Clearinghouse on Languages and Linguistics through the following contract:

U.S. Department of Education
Office of Educational Research and Improvement/Institute of Education Sciences
National Library of Education
Contract No. ED-99-CO-0008

The opinions expressed in this publication are those of the authors and do not necessarily reflect the positions or policies of any office of the U.S. Department of Education.

Library of Congress Cataloging-in-Publication Data

Short, Deborah
    Creating access : language and academic programs for secondary school newcomers/Deborah J. Short, Beverly A. Boyson.
        p. cm.
    Includes bibliographical references.
    ISBN 1-887744-87-8 (alk. paper)
        1. English language—Study and teaching (Secondary)—Foreign speakers. 2. Interdisciplinary approach in education. I. Boyson, Beverly A. (Beverly Ann). II. Title.

PE1128.A2S565 2004
424'.0071'2—dc22   2004040750

Creating Access

Language and Academic Programs
for Secondary School Newcomers

Deborah J. Short
Beverly A. Boyson

CAL

CAL

Center for Applied Linguistics

CAL's mission is to improve communication through better understanding of language and culture. CAL's staff of educators and researchers are dedicated to promoting and improving the teaching and learning of languages, identifying and solving problems related to language and culture, and serving as a resource for information about language and culture. CAL's activities include research, teacher education, analysis and dissemination of information, development of instructional materials and language assessments, technical assistance, program evaluation, and policy analysis. CAL is a private, nonprofit organization.

Educational Resources Information Center
Clearinghouse on Languages and Linguistics
(ERIC/CLL)

From 1966 through 2003, ERIC operated as a nationwide information network whose aim was to improve educational practice by providing ready access to current education literature. Through its system of decentralized, subject-specific clearinghouses, ERIC developed and maintained the world's largest database of education-related materials, offered extensive question-answering services, and produced and distributed a wide range of publications designed to provide ready access to important information on topics in education. ERIC/CLL, which was operated by the Center for Applied Linguistics from 1974 through 2003 with funding from the U.S. Department of Education, focused on topics in foreign language education, English as a second language, bilingual education, and all areas of linguistics. As the result of decisions by the Department of Education, all ERIC clearinghouses ceased operations as of December 31, 2003.

Delta Systems Co., Inc., is a publisher and distributor of ESL and foreign language materials. Since 1993, Delta has had a co-publishing agreement with the Center for Applied Linguistics. Joint CAL/Delta publications include the *Language in Education: Theory and Practice* series of professional reference books and the *Topics in Immigrant Education* series. Delta and CAL's most recent joint venture is the *Professional Practice Series,* of which this book is the third volume.

Table of Contents

The Professional Practice Series

Like so many people in today's fast-paced world, teachers and education administrators are exceedingly busy. In addition to working with students in the classroom and designing and overseeing educational programs, they are likely to be involved in a host of other activities: curriculum development; design and development of instructional materials; committee assignments; coordination of afterschool activities; and communication with parents, counselors, community leaders, and others involved in the education of their students. In addition, they need to stay abreast of new research and developments in their subject areas and in the field of education. Reading the literature, attending conferences, and participating in and leading workshops and in-service training sessions are all part of their ongoing professional development.

Teachers and administrators need ready access to clear and reliable information about effective practices in language education. The *Professional Practice Series,* developed by the ERIC Clearinghouse on Languages and Linguistics and published by the Center for Applied Linguistics and Delta Systems, is designed to provide practitioners with current information on topics, trends, and techniques in language teaching. Each volume begins with an overview of the topic and the chapters in the book. Each chapter focuses on a particular aspect of the topic and the knowledge we have about it. The chapters describe the strategies and techniques used by effective teachers and administrators and offer practical guidelines and suggestions to help others implement similar strategies in their own classrooms, schools, and districts. Each volume closes with a summary of key points in the book and general guidelines and recommendations.

It is our hope that the *Professional Practice Series* will provide language educators with accessible, timely information, supported by theory and research, that will help them improve or enhance their teaching and their programs.

Jeanne Rennie and Joy Kreeft Peyton, Series Editors
Center for Applied Linguistics
Washington, DC

For online information about this series and other books included in it, visit www.practiceseries.com.

Acknowledgments

We would like to express our appreciation to the staff of the 115 secondary newcomer programs who participated in our CREDE research study and in particular, the staff of César Chávez Multicultural Academic Center, Liberty High School, International Newcomer Academy, and Township High School District 214 for opening their doors to us. We are grateful for the support and help of our colleagues at CAL, including Thom Raybold, Luan Nguyen, and Huy Nguyen for constructing and updating the newcomer database; Chris Montone for the initial survey design; Jeanne Rennie and Elizabeth Peterson for editorial expertise; and Leonida Vizcarra, Shannon Fitzsimmons, and Bronwyn Coltrane for research and administrative assistance. Thanks are extended as well to the anonymous reviewers of this monograph for their insightful suggestions.

In 2002-2003, the students at the Newcomer Center in Township High School District 214, Illinois, represented seven countries and four languages: Spanish, Korean, Chinese, and Polish.

Introduction to Secondary School Newcomer Students and Programs

The impact this program has had on our students is that they become knowledgeable about procedures, rules, and expectations within our school system. They become familiar with cultural differences and similarities, social registers, and protocol, and become functional in a non-threatening environment. They acquire beginning conversational and academic English and receive academic instruction.

—Learning Enrichment and Academic Program
in Wenatchee (WA) School District

Across the nation's school districts, the number of students from non-English-speaking backgrounds has risen dramatically. They represent the fastest growing segment of the student population by a wide margin. From 1991–1992 through 2001–2002, the number of limited English proficient (LEP) students in public schools grew by 95%, while total enrollment increased only 12%. In at least 15 states, the enrollment of LEP students grew 200% (National Clearinghouse for English Language Acquisition, 2002). Nationwide, 35% of LEP students were enrolled in the middle grades (Grades 4–8), and 19% were enrolled in high school (Grades 9–12).

The rise in immigrant students conforms to the increase in the overall immigrant population in the United States. The U.S. Census Bureau determined that in 1999, 20% of school-age children had at least one parent who was an immigrant, and 5% of the students were immigrants themselves (Jamieson, Curry, & Martinez, 2001). However, when race or ethnic origin is considered, the distinctions among students become more apparent. Sixty-five percent of Hispanic students and 88% of Asian and Pacific Islander students had at least one immigrant parent. According to *Latinos in Education* (1999), a report published by the White House Initiative on Educational Excellence for Hispanic Americans, Hispanic students make up 75% of all students in English as a second language (ESL), bilingual, and other English language support programs.

According to researchers Ruiz-de-Velasco & Fix (2000), the geographic distribution of immigrants is concentrated in urban areas, primarily in six states that account for three fourths of all immigrant children: California (35%), Texas (11.3%), New York (11%), Florida (6.7%), Illinois (5%), and New Jersey (4%). However, the number of immigrant children in states that are not among the top six increased by 40%, from 1.5 million to 2.1 million, between 1990 and 1995. The researchers found that these states were less likely than the top six to deliver language instruction and other services that recent immigrant students need.

They also found a serious disparity between distribution of language resources and the grade-level distribution of immigrant children. A higher percentage of foreign-born immigrants attend secondary schools than elementary schools, yet spending on language acquisition programs tends to be concentrated in elementary schools. As a result, a significantly smaller proportion of secondary school English language learners receive language support services, creating a mismatch between the number and needs of immigrant middle and high school students and the resources targeted for them (Ruiz-de-Velasco & Fix, 2000).

From a socioeconomic perspective, newcomers are more likely to be poor than other youth (Waggoner, 1999). The poverty rate among foreign-born immigrants and their families has tripled since 1970 (Ruiz-de-Velasco & Fix, 2000). A number of newcomer youth are undocumented, and this affects their socioeconomic status. These youth may attend school, but they often face significant barriers to working and to attending public postsecondary educational institutions after they graduate or leave school.

Although immigrants students have better attendance rates on average than U.S.-born students, their dropout rates are higher (Ruiz-de-Velasco & Fix, 2000; Waggoner, 1999). Hispanics have the highest dropout rate of any ethnic or racial group. In 1998, 30% of all Hispanics aged 16-24 dropped out of school. For blacks, the rate was 14%, less than half the Hispanic rate; for whites, it was 8%, almost four times less. Of particular note is that the dropout rate for immigrant Hispanics was 44%, more than double the 21% rate of native-born Hispanics (*Latinos in Education*, 1999).

Some of the higher dropout rates among newcomers can be attributed to the over-age status of a subset of this population. Across metropolitan areas of the United States, over-age, underschooled youth aged 17-21 are enrolling in public schools in greater numbers than before (see, e.g., Dufresne & Hall, 1997; Gonzalez, 1994; New York State Education Department, 1997; Olsen, Jaramillo, McCall-Perez, & White, 1999). Many of these students fail to meet graduation requirements before their age forces them out of free public education.

However, some over-age newcomer students do not intend to graduate from high school but seek educational opportunities for a limited time to develop English skills or find a pathway into a General Education Development (GED) program. The New York State Education Department (NYSED) held a series of symposia for educators of these students sponsored by the Office of Bilingual Education. A resulting publication (New York State Department of Education, 1997) offers guidance to educators on how to identify over-age students with interrupted schooling and discusses alternatives to the traditional academic track for a high school diploma.

Newcomer Students in the United States

Not all immigrant students have limited English proficiency, but many of them do. These English language learners come to U.S. schools with many resources to share, including linguistic resources in their native language. But not all English language learners are alike. They enter U.S. schools with a wide range of language proficiencies (in English and in their native language) and subject matter knowledge. They differ in their educational backgrounds, expectations of schooling, socioeconomic status, age of arrival in the United States, and personal experiences coming to and living in the United States.

Among immigrant students, some English language learners (ELLs) have strong academic preparation. They are at or above the age-appropriate grade level in the school curricula, and they are literate in their native language. Their primary need is for English language development, so that as they become more proficient in English, they can transfer their educational knowledge to the courses they are taking in the United States. They may need to focus extra attention on subjects such as U.S. history, which they may not have studied previously. These students have the greatest likelihood of achieving educational success if they receive appropriate language and content instruction in their schools.

Other immigrant students arrive at U.S. schools with significant gaps in their educational backgrounds. Their schooling may have been interrupted for reasons of war or other military conflict, isolated locales that cannot attract full-time teachers, or seasonal agricultural demands, among other reasons. In some countries, adolescent students are only required to attend school part time. Public education in parts of Mexico, Central America, and the Caribbean can end after sixth grade.

Often these underschooled students, particularly in middle and high school, are placed several grade levels below their age cohorts. Ruiz-de-Velasco & Fix (2000) found that 20% of all limited English proficient (LEP) students at the high school level and 12% at the middle school level had missed 2 or more years of schooling since age 6. Among Hispanic students age 15-17, more than one third are enrolled below the usual grade level for their age (Jamieson, Curry, & Martinez, 2001). For many secondary LEP students in Hayward, California, researchers found a difference of more than 1 year between age-appropriate placement and the number of years of schooling completed (Olsen et al.,1999). Most of the underschooled students could not read or write in their primary language or had very weak literacy skills, and they were 3 or more years below grade level in mathematics.

Newcomer students with limited formal schooling and below-grade-level literacy are most at risk for educational failure. These students have weak literacy skills in their native language, lack English language skills and knowledge in specific subject areas, and often need additional time to become accustomed to school routines and expectations in the United States. They are entering U.S. schools with weak academic skills at a time when schools are emphasizing rigorous, standards-based curricula and high-stakes assessments for all students in order to meet the requirements of the No Child Left Behind Act (NCLB) of 2001. NCLB requires all schools receiving Title I funds to administer annual tests of reading and mathematics to all students in Grades 3-8. English language learners must be included in these tests. NCLB also requires annual assessment of the English language development of all students designated as limited English proficient and who are enrolled in programs receiving Title I or III funds. Nineteen states require students to pass high school proficiency or end-of-course exams before they can receive a diploma. Additional states are developing such assessments and will roll them out over the next few years (Doherty & Skinner, 2003). Given the limited English skills of newcomers, these high stakes tests are more likely to reflect their English knowledge than their content knowledge (Coltrane, 2002; Menken, 2000). They place particular pressure on secondary school newcomer students who have limited time to learn English, take the required content courses, and catch up to their native-English-speaking peers before graduation.

The underachievement of secondary school newcomer students has prompted educators and researchers to identify student-specific needs that programs should address. Literacy skill development is one critical area for targeted educational support, especially literacy strategies that are developmentally appropriate for adolescents (Hamayan, 1994; Moran, Stobbe, Tinajero, & Tinajero, 1993; Olsen et al., 1999). The high dropout rates and underperformance on assessments clearly indicate that bridging gaps in the newcomer students' educational backgrounds is another important area for attention (Olsen et al., 1999). The creation of courses like the *Fast Math* program in Fairfax County, Virginia (Helman & Buchanan, 1993), which can help students gain several years' worth of instruction in one subject area in 6 months to a year, is crucial to help newcomer students catch up to their native-English-speaking classmates who have been in the U.S. school system for all their educational lives.

Another educational need frequently cited is helping students become acclimated to their new community and to schooling in the United States. Several researchers have reported the isolation and confusion newcomer students feel in their schools upon arrival and sometimes well into the first year (Cheng, 1999; Dufresne & Hall, 1997; Gonzalez, 1994; Moran, Stobbe, Tinajero & Tinajero, 1993; Olsen, 2000; Olsen et al., 1999; Pilon, 1993; Te, 1997). These students are linguistically isolated because they do not yet speak English and may speak a native language not spoken by other students or staff. They may be culturally isolated because as immigrants they are not familiar with American traditions, school practices (e.g., rooting for sports teams, changing clothes for gym in a locker room), and popular culture for teenagers (e.g., television shows, music, clothing). Some students have felt ridiculed by English speakers because of their lack of English proficiency and unfortunately shun their native language, resulting in an unnecessary loss of bilingual resources (Olsen, 2000).

This book has been written for educators who want to create greater access for newcomer students to the academic curriculum and the world beyond school. The purpose of this book is to introduce readers to newcomer programs and provide information and guidance to schools that are seeking to develop and implement a newcomer program or to improve an existing one. It describes the results of a 4-year research project that documented middle and high school newcomer programs around the United States through survey and case study methodologies. The researchers defined newcomer students as follows: "Recent immigrant students who have very limited or no English language proficiency and who may have had limited formal education in their native countries."

In the first national study of its kind, researchers documented the range of program designs and implementation features in operation. Newcomer programs are a fairly recent phenomenon, established to help reduce the underachievement of newcomers. Most programs seek at a minimum to provide students with a strong foundation in social and academic English language skills and acculturation to U.S. schools and educational expectations so that they may be successful in school and be prepared eventually for college or the world of work.

Language and Academic Programs for Recent Immigrants: A Research Study

In 1996, the National Center for Research on Education, Diversity & Excellence (CREDE)[1] funded researchers at the Center for Applied Linguistics (CAL) to conduct the first national research project to study secondary-level newcomer programs. The goals of this 4-year research project were twofold: (1) to identify and document secondary newcomer programs in school districts around the United States and (2) to

---

[1] CREDE is a national research and development center funded by the U.S. Department of Education, Institute of Education Sciences, National Institute for the Education of At-Risk Students. CREDE is operated by the University of California, Santa Cruz, in collaboration with 26 institutions across the United States.

examine more closely several of the programs for evidence of their effectiveness and to identify the ways in which they promote newcomers' transitions into U.S. schools. The study defined a newcomer program in the following way: "A program that, in a special academic environment for a limited period of time, educates recent immigrant students who have no or very limited English language proficiency and who may have had limited formal education in their native countries." However, the research revealed that the definition of a newcomer program varies widely across the sites studied. These differences are discussed later in this chapter.

Research Questions

In order to examine the operation of newcomer programs in depth, the study investigated the following questions:

1. a) What models of secondary newcomer programs are currently in practice?
   b) What are the goals of the newcomer programs?
   c) What distinguishes newcomer programs from traditional bilingual and ESL programs at home schools (i.e., the school in a student's designated attendance area)?
2. What are the characteristics of these programs, and what background sociocultural features determine and support them? (e.g., identification, placement, and assessment of students; teacher background and training; comprehensive social and health services; length of program)
3. a) How do schools integrate newcomer students with other students in the school system?
   b) What transition practices are in place to facilitate the newcomer students' exit from the newcomer program into the home schools, and how do schools monitor newcomer students once they have entered the home schools?
4. How do newcomer programs compare with traditional bilingual or ESL programs in terms of attendance and dropout rates, English language growth, content area growth, attitudes toward school, and postsecondary options?

Data Collection and Analysis

Initially, we identified possible sites of newcomer programs through

- a review of the literature and Title VII proposals;
- state and local district contacts;
- federal contacts at the U.S. Department of Education; and
- calls for nominations posted on educational listservs, on the Center for Applied Linguistics' Web site, in professional newsletters, and at professional conferences.

After the first year of the project, dissemination activities such as conference presentations, publications, and interviews with journalists resulted in more program nominations.

We contacted all the nominated sites to determine if they had secondary newcomer programs that matched our research definition. For those that did, we collected data through survey questionnaires and phone interviews. The first survey was developed to collect data from the programs for the 1996–1997 school year. The survey gathered information on program design, student demographics, features of instruction and assessment, program staffing, and other services. It also asked about the literacy strategies used with newcomer students and the transition of students from the newcomer program to other programs in the district. As we learned more about the program models, we revised the survey in each of the 3 additional project years (1997–1998, 1998–1999, 1999–2000) to elicit more data that would reflect the features of the wide variety of newcomer programs.

As completed questionnaires were returned, the data were verified and entered into a research database. Data were analyzed, and profiles of the programs were prepared for publication each year of the study in a directory or supplemental volume. At the end of the research study, the *Directory of Secondary Newcomer Programs in the United States: Revised 2000* (Short & Boyson, 2000) was published. The profiles were also placed in a searchable, online database on the Web (www.cal.org/ newcomerdb) to provide access to researchers and practitioners in the field.

In addition, researchers conducted site visits at several program locations and conducted case studies at a select few. The site visits allowed us to further confirm the information we were receiving from the survey questionnaires. The case study component of the project enabled us to investigate more closely the implementation of a small number of newcomer programs, the achievement of students in the programs, and their transition out of the newcomer program into other schools or academic programs. Data were gathered from classroom observations and from interviews with program administrators, teachers, and students. Program literature—brochures, parent guides, assessment tools, curriculum frameworks—was collected. Data from the case study site visits were organized by analytic categories (e.g., grade levels served, students' native languages, instructional program design) and examined to describe similarities and differences across sites.

As of the 1999–2000 school year, newcomer programs in 29 states and the District of Columbia had participated in our research study. During the 1999-2000 school year, we recorded 115 programs operating at 196 sites, serving students from more than 600 middle schools and high schools. Table 1.1 shows the breakdown of program location by state, identifying the number of programs and program sites in each state, and further indicating which grade levels are served at the different sites (middle school, high school, or middle and high school combined). Almost 75% of the programs in our database have been established since 1990. Over 50% of the programs are located in four states: California, New Jersey, New York, and Texas.

TABLE **1.1**■

Number of Programs Profiled in Directory 2000	115
Number of Program Sites	196
Number of States Reporting Programs	30

States	Programs	Sites	Middle School Sites	High School Sites	Middle & High Sites
Alaska	1	1	0	0	1
California	15	17	5	11	1
Colorado	1	1	0	1	0
Connecticut	2	2	1	1	0
District of Columbia	1	1	0	1	0
Florida	1	8	6	2	0
Georgia	2	3	0	0	3
Illinois	4	4	2	2	0
Iowa	3	2	0	1	1
Kansas	3	3	0	2	1
Maryland	3	19	9	10	0
Massachusetts	2	2	1	1	0
Michigan	2	3	1	1	1
Minnesota	4	4	1	3	0
Missouri	2	2	1	1	0
Nebraska	1	1	0	0	1
Nevada	2	18	8	10	0
New Jersey	12	13	5	7	1
New Mexico	1	1	0	1	0
New York	15	15	5	10	0
North Carolina	4	4	0	3	1
Ohio	1	2	1	1	0
Oklahoma	1	1	0	1	0
Oregon	3	4	1	1	2
Pennsylvania	2	2	0	2	0
Texas	17	44	19	22	3
Utah	1	1	0	1	0
Virginia	1	1	0	1	0
Washington	6	10	4	5	1
Wisconsin	2	7	4	3	0
Totals	**115**	**196**	**74**	**105**	**17**

Newcomer programs are found in many types of communities across the United States, although most are located in urban settings, where the greatest number of newcomer students reside. In recent years, however, newcomers are found increasingly in suburban and rural areas as well. Among the 115 programs profiled in 1999-2000, 76% were in urban metropolitan areas, 17% were in suburbs, and 7% were rural. This indicates that newcomer programs offer a viable option for all types of districts in the United States if they have the requisite student population.

More than half of the programs (62) in the project database serve high school students. Twenty-six programs serve middle school students; the remainder (27) provide instruction to both middle and high school students. The fact that more high school than middle school programs are in operation is related to one rationale for this model: High school immigrant students, especially older adolescents, need targeted intervention strategies beyond traditional ESL and bilingual programs to accelerate their learning so they may be able to graduate in the limited time available to them.

The matrix in Appendix A identifies the 115 newcomer programs in the study, their locations, and key features, such as school level, program enrollment, and type of instruction offered. Chapter 2 offers a complete discussion of the range of program features.

Program Evaluation

The research project reviewed available literature on newcomer programs and found very few studies that evaluated programs. A few case studies and some comparisons of instructional practices across programs are available (Bush, 1992; Constantino & Lavadenz, 1993; Olsen et al., 1999), but overall this program type has received scant attention. It has been reported in the limited literature (Barton, personal communication, 1995; Chang, 1990; McDonnell & Hill, 1993; Olsen & Dowell, 1989) that the newcomer program class size is usually smaller than at other schools; the faculty is often hand-picked and actively involved in school governance; close connections exist among students, their families, and the community; field trips are common to help students learn about community resources; and the curricula may be specially designed for the program. One report that did try to evaluate newcomer programs from a cost-effectiveness perspective offered a qualified endorsement of newcomer schools:

> *Although they too are constrained by the limited supply of bilingual teachers, newcomer schools provide a more focused alternative that ensures recent immigrants fortunate enough to be enrolled in them with a richly integrated educational experience, at least for a short time.* (McDonnell & Hill, 1993, p. 97)

In our research design, we had hoped to assess the effectiveness of newcomer programs vis-à-vis other language support models. We were unable to do so because the districts did not identify the students as newcomers in their district assessment systems and therefore did not examine their data separately to determine newcomer students' progress compared to the progress of English language learners who did not enter the newcomer program. While we did find some evidence of student language and academic growth in newcomer programs (e.g., in pre- and posttest scores, in Title VII reports submitted to the U.S. Department of Education, in anecdotal data from staff), almost none of the programs identified the newcomer students as such in their school accountability databases after they made the transition out of the program. This rendered the academic tracking of program graduates impossible, and we could not compare how well they were doing in school with other English language learners who had not been in the newcomer program. However, as a result of our survey and interview questions and a desire to provide evidence of the program's worth to policymakers, some programs have begun to identify the students for evaluative purposes. Future research should analyze and interpret these data to make determinations as to the effectiveness of this program model.

Rationale and Overview of Newcomer Programs

Our research uncovered practical and theoretical reasons for the establishment of newcomer programs. Traditional English as a second language (ESL) and bilingual education programs are not designed to serve the specific needs of newcomers, in part because at the secondary level, curricula and materials are predicated on the belief that students have literacy skills and are acculturated to school. Temporary strategies, such as placing students in grades lower than their age cohorts, have been unsuccessful and are developmentally inappropriate (Olsen et al., 1999). To bridge the gap between newcomers' needs and regular language support programs, this relatively new model, the newcomer program, has been developed and is growing in use across the United States.

We found that existing newcomer programs vary in their definition of newcomers. Some define the students by their length of residency in the United States, their English language proficiency, their test scores, and/or their age. More than three fourths of the programs define newcomers as recent immigrants to the United States with limited proficiency in English, while one seventh define these students as new only to the district. The length of time that students have been in the United States is a factor in about one fourth of the programs, as is student age. One tenth of the programs define newcomers as those students with test scores on an English proficiency exam that fall below a specified threshold.

The rationale for establishing newcomer programs differed somewhat across the sites, but several specific considerations and beliefs have influenced the decision to set up this type of program:

- The literacy needs of English language learners can be addressed more effectively in newcomer classes than in a classroom that includes both literate and nonliterate students.

- A welcoming and nurturing environment is beneficial to older immigrant students (i.e., those of secondary school age, generally 12–21 years old) who may have limited prior experience with schooling.
- Gaps in the educational backgrounds of middle and high school immigrant students can be filled more readily, and learning of core academic skills and knowledge can be accelerated in the newcomer program.
- The chances of educational success for newcomer students are enhanced when connections between the school and students' families and communities are established and reinforced.

Districts have therefore developed newcomer programs that offer a set of courses distinct from the regular language support programs to address the unique needs of students with no or low English proficiency, low literacy, and limited formal schooling. The main objectives of newcomer programs are to help students acquire beginning English skills, provide some instruction in core academic content areas, and guide the students' acculturation to the U.S. school system. Many programs have additional objectives, such as developing the students' native language skills and acclimating them to their new community. Overall, the goal of most programs is to accelerate the students' learning so they can make the transition to other school programs and be prepared for the literacy and content demands of bilingual, ESL, or mainstream courses.

Although the goals for newcomer programs appear similar to goals of other language support programs, there are distinguishing characteristics that reflect the newcomer program philosophy.

1. Not all students learning English as an additional language are eligible for a newcomer program. These programs are primarily designed for those students with the weakest English and academic skills, those who enter school several months after the academic year has begun, or those who are older learners (e.g., 17 years old or above).
2. Most newcomer programs limit enrollment to one to three semesters of instruction.[2] This policy is in place partly to ensure that new-

---

[2] As will be described later, a few programs do offer a full 4-year high school or 3-year middle school.

comer students are not segregated from the main student body for their academic careers and partly because newcomer programs aim to bridge gaps in students' educational backgrounds.

3. A number of course offerings are distinct from the regular ESL or bilingual education programs, such as native language literacy development, orientation to school and the community, and foundational content courses (e.g., arithmetic, introduction to U.S. history).

4. Newcomer programs help the students learn a range of school skills, depending on their age, backgrounds, and needs, for example, how to hold a pencil, how to follow a high school schedule, how to negotiate the city transportation system, how to read textbooks, how to solve mathematics problems and perform science experiments, and more.

5. These programs involve the families in the range of services they offer. More than just encouraging parents to attend school meetings, newcomer program staff reach out to help families access social, health, and employment services, often through school-community partnerships established for these purposes.

It should be mentioned that newcomer programs have generated some controversy in certain communities around the United States and in Canada. Some educators and residents have expressed concern about the segregation of these students from the main student body. This concern is often answered by pointing out that these students are already isolated for linguistic and cultural reasons and do not typically interact with more proficient ESL/bilingual students or native-English-speaking students during their first 6 months to a year in school. Further, the programs are of limited duration, are mostly organized as programs within schools, and are voluntary. Proponents believe a newcomer program offers the students the best opportunity to learn English, develop content knowledge, and become acculturated to U.S. practices so they can more successfully integrate with other students in school. In a few instances, the U.S. Department of Education's Office of Civil Rights has been asked to look into these programs (Belluck, 1995). In all cases, the programs have been allowed to continue, although they have been encouraged to seek extracurricular opportunities for interaction with non-newcomer students.

Summary

According to the research conducted for this project, changing student demographics, education standards, and accountability directives spurred the development of newcomer programs in the 1990s. Schools and districts established these programs to offer the educational benefits of accelerated, intensive attention to language and content skills that help students prepare for the regular curriculum, through a supportive environment that creates close ties to families and the community. Specific program goals may vary, but most programs have been designed to accelerate the students' social and academic English language development and acculturation to U.S. schools and educational expectations. The programs strive to create better access to the educational system for these students so they may be successful in school and prepare for postsecondary college or work opportunities.

This book showcases the commonalities and differences across secondary school newcomer programs. In chapter 1, we have provided a brief introduction to newcomer students and programs and described a 4-year study of newcomer programs in the United States. Chapter 2 presents findings from the survey research conducted on this programmatic model and describes the options for design features. Chapter 3 explains the reasons that programs choose certain designs and offers guidance on establishing a newcomer program. Chapter 4 describes several case study examples of successful program implementation. The book concludes with chapter 5, a discussion of the trends seen in newcomer programs during the course of the research and directions for future research, policy, and practice.

Students at Newcomers High School in New York study biology using hands-on activities that promote the learning of content and language in sheltered instruction classrooms.

Secondary Newcomer Programs in the United States: Survey Findings

The half-day pullout model is proving to be an efficient, cost-effective way to deliver newcomer services in our district. The program is housed in a centrally located vocational center with district transportation already in place. Administrative backing has been strong, providing good facilities, computers and Internet access, recruitment of experienced staff, and advanced planning. Testing and assessment for initial placement are effectively indicating student strengths and weaknesses. Students receive three and a half credits per semester in core subjects, usually a combination of English and U.S. or world history. Once students complete a year of core courses, they transition back to their home school's ESL classes.

—Bilingual Newcomer Center, Anchorage (AK) School District

No unified model for a newcomer program has emerged. Newcomer program designs vary across sites in terms of educational goals, site options, length of program enrollment, length of daily contact, instructional and assessment practices, staffing, parent involvement, and resource allocation (Chang, 1990; Friedlander, 1991; McDonnell & Hill, 1993; Olsen & Dowell, 1989). The survey distributed to the 115 middle and high school programs in our study gathered information on all of these features of newcomer programs. This chapter presents survey data results, thus providing an overview of the various ways in which newcomer programs have been implemented. It is hoped that this will help new and existing programs make informed choices from among the variety of options available for program design and implementation.

Newcomer Students
Definition and Entry Criteria

Although the programs studied in this project vary in their definition of newcomers, most programs include recent arrival to the United States and limited or no English proficiency as defining characteristics that distinguish their students from other ESL and bilingual education students. Entry criteria that have been specified in the programs are listed below. The percentage in parentheses indicates the percentage of the 115 programs in this study that include the item among their criteria.

- Lack of English language skills (93%)
- Low native language literacy skills (49%)
- Length of time in the United States (64%—some specifying 1 year or less, others less than 2 or 3 years)
- English language test scores below a specified threshold (10%)
- Age, parental preference, recommendation of a teacher or committee, and other criteria

In all of the school districts, entry into the newcomer program is voluntary.

Student Demographics

The 115 newcomer programs in our study enrolled close to 15,000 middle and high school students during the 1999-2000 school year. Most were recent immigrants to the United States; some were refugees. Their ages ranged from 10 to 26 years. In 85% of the programs, 80-100% of the students were eligible for the free/reduced-price lunch program. Over 60% of the students in newcomer programs lived in three states: California, New York, and Texas. Other states that had large numbers of newcomer students were Minnesota, Nevada, and New Jersey.

The newcomer students came from more than 90 countries and spoke more than 60 languages. Spanish speakers predominated (there were Spanish speakers in 95% of the programs), but most of the programs served students from a variety of language backgrounds. There were Vietnamese speakers in 38% of the programs and Somali speakers in 22%. Other frequently served groups were speakers of Mandarin, Pilipino, Russian, Haitian Creole, Polish, Punjabi, Hindi, and Bengali. Results from the surveys revealed that four or more native languages were represented in 52% of the programs.

Students in newcomer programs are native speakers of many languages: Afrikaans, Albanian, Amharic, Arabic, Bengali, Bosnian, Bulgarian, Cambodian, Cantonese, Chaldean, Chinese, Cree, Croatian, Dinka (Sudanese), English Creole, Farsi, Finnish, French, French Creole, Fujianese, Fukienese, German, Gujarati, Haitian Creole, Hindi, Hmong, Ibo, Japanese, Korean, Krio, Kurdish, Lao, Lingala, Lithuanian, Mabaan, Malay dialects (Sindhi, Mandigo), Mandarin, Mixteco, Nuer, Oromo, Oti, Pilipino, Polish, Portuguese, Punjabi, Romanian, Russian, Serbo-Croatian, Somali, Spanish, Sudanese, Swahili, Tagalog, Thai, Tigrinya, Ukranian, Urdu, Vietnamese, and varieties of English (Caribbean, Ghanaian, Jamaican, Liberian, Nigerian).

Changes in Student Population Over Time

Newcomer programs may experience change from year to year in the demographics of their student body, often having to do with the kind of immigrant patterns the United States is experiencing. In the 1999–2000 survey, 37% of the programs reported that they had experienced a shift in their student populations over the course of the years they had been in operation. In most sites where change occurred, the student populations had become more diverse with regard to the number of languages spoken and the number of countries represented. Fifteen percent of the programs reported that the number of students with little formal education had increased and that more over-age students had enrolled in recent years. A few schools mentioned that the religious orientation of the student population had changed. Some sites reported striking changes in population over time; for example, Bosnian refugee students have replaced Vietnamese refugee students in Fort Worth, Texas.

Program Models
Program Site

When districts decide to develop a newcomer program, location is an issue that must be addressed early in the planning process. Space and transportation are among the key issues to consider. Among the 115 programs in our study, there are basically three site models: program within a school, separate site, and whole school (4-year high schools). Each of these models is described below.

Program Within a School

The most common model across the newcomer sites, found in more than 75% of the programs, is a program that is located within the larger school setting. In this model, newcomer students are served in their home school (as per designated attendance area), where they have opportunities to interact with mainstream students for part of the day in classes such as physical education, music, and art, or during extracurricular activities. Some programs organize specific activities for the newcomer students to work cooperatively with mainstream students on school or community projects, thus providing opportunities for meaningful interaction between the newcomers and fluent speakers of English.

Newcomer students in 64% of the programs within a school remain in the program for 1 year or less, while students in other programs may remain for more than 1 year. Many of the students who exit from this type of newcomer program remain at the same school to continue their studies in the regular language support program, which may offer ESL or bilingual services. Other students may attend another district school upon exit from the newcomer program.

Separate Site

Seventeen percent of the newcomer programs in our study are housed in a separate location—sometimes a former school building that had been closed due to a decline in student population, sometimes space that has been leased or purchased by the district. This option allows districts to consolidate resources by serving all of their newcomer students at a single site. More than half of the separate-site programs (11 out of 19) operate for a full day. Two of the full-day, separate-site programs are located at district intake centers, where all language minority students are assessed and placed. When instruction is provided for students at the intake centers, it is usually for a brief period of time after arrival, for orientation to U.S. schools and intensive English language courses. Students enrolled in newcomer programs at intake centers remain there for a range of 4 to 18 weeks.

In seven of the separate-site programs, students spend a portion of the day in their home schools and are transported to the newcomer program for a half day or less of specialized instruction. In one separate-site program, students may attend for a half day or a full day, depending on their individual needs. Most students who attend separate site programs remain for 1 year or less. Three of the separate-site programs allow students to remain for more than 1 year if they are over age for their grade level and have low literacy skills in their native language.

Whole School

The least common newcomer program model, represented by 6% of the programs in our study, is the whole-school model, developed primarily for high school students. Six of the seven whole-school programs are 4-year high schools offering a curriculum that leads to graduation. One school offers a Grade 6–8 and a Grade 9–12 program. Some whole-school programs are designed specifically for students who have experienced interrupted schooling or who lack formal education in their native language and are over age for their grade level. Students in these schools may remain in the program until graduation, or they may transfer to the regular ESL, bilingual, or mainstream program at another high school.

Figure 2.1 illustrates the distribution of program site models in our study.

FIGURE **2.1** ■

▨	Programs within a school	77%
▨	Separate site	17%
▦	Whole school	6%

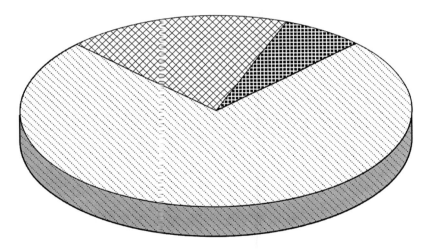

Program Sites

The selection of a program site must take into consideration the number of students to be served and their school attendance areas. In 65% of the programs studied, students from more than one school came to the newcomer program site; 25% served students from only one school. In the remaining 10%, students were assigned to a newcomer program at the district intake center.

Two programs served students from more than one school district: One middle school program in New York City served two school districts, and an alternative middle and high school in Michigan served students from five districts. One reason for creating programs that extend across districts is to pool resources and constitute a reasonably sized student body. This arrangement might also occur when one district has an existing program and a neighboring district has only a few students who need to be served.

Length of Daily Program

Depending on the resources available and on the students being served, a newcomer program may involve one or two course periods, half the school day, or the full school day. Fifty-six percent of the programs in our study offer full-day instruction. This full-day schedule provides time to offer several content area courses along with English language instruction. It conforms with the trend to accelerate student learning across multiple content areas to help students develop the skills and background knowledge they need for the enhanced academic rigor of other school programs. In the case of high-school-age students, a full-day program accommodates the restricted span of time they may have to participate in public education if they seek a high school diploma.

As shown in Table 2.1 (page 26), 17% of the programs are designed with a half-day schedule, sometimes to accommodate two groups of students at one site (e.g., middle school students in the morning, high school students in the afternoon), sometimes to promote interaction

TABLE **2.1** ■

Daily enrollment	# of programs	Percentage of programs	# of students	Percentage of students
Full day	65	56%	9,580	65%
Half day	19	17%	2,100	14%
Less than half day	7	6%	306	2%
Afterschool	2	2%	280	2%
Combination	22	19%	2,495	17%

Student Population According to Length of Daily Enrollment in
Newcomer Programs in 1999-2000

between newcomers and other students at the school. Fourteen percent of the students are in half-day programs. Six percent of the programs in our study offer newcomer courses for less than half of the school day—that is, for one to three class periods. Two percent of the programs operate solely after school, and students attend on a voluntary basis. The less-than-half-day and afterschool programs each serve 2% of the students. Nineteen percent of the programs offer more than one option. For example, some programs operate for the full day as well as after school, and a few operate for a half day in addition to after school. Table 2.1 above shows the distribution of programs and students among the various daily program models.

Length of Program Enrollment

Figure 2.2 (page 27) illustrates the length of time on average that students remain in newcomer programs. The length of enrollment is usually determined on an individual basis, according to the student's linguistic and academic needs. However, many programs set a maximum time that students may remain in the program, and although

FIGURE **2.2**■

▦	Less than 1 school year	6%
▦	1 school year only	43%
▧	1 year and more than 1 year options	23%
▨	More than 1 year	28%

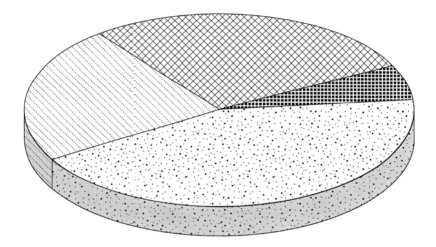

Length of Enrollment in Program

some students may exit early, no one remains beyond the maximum time limit. Six percent of the programs studied in 1999–2000 were designed to educate students for less than 1 school year, 43% for 1 school year only, and 28% for more than 1 school year. The remaining 23% served some of their students for 1 school year and others for more than 1 year (including the 1 school year plus summer programs), depending on the students' individual needs.

Student Enrollment by Program Type
Figure 2.3 (page 29) shows the approximate number of students enrolled across newcomer program types. Five percent of the students were enrolled in programs that last for less than 1 school year, 24% were enrolled in programs that last for 1 school year only, and 41% were enrolled in programs lasting longer than 1 year for all students. The remaining 30% were enrolled in programs that last for 1 school year or more (i.e., programs that last 1 school year plus summer and programs designated 1 year or more depending on individual students' needs).

The number of students served in the programs ranged from 7 students at one site in New Jersey to more than 1,000 at a high school in New York City. Fifty-five percent of the programs enrolled 50 or more students; about 35% of them served 100 or more students.

Program Features
Grade Levels Served
The grade levels served in newcomer programs vary widely, often to accommodate the students' specific needs and the needs of the districts' other language support and academic programs. Some sites served all grade levels in the school's category (e.g., Grades 6–8 for middle school, Grades 9–12 for high school). A number of programs combined middle school and high school students in one location but did not co-mingle the two levels, except perhaps for a basic literacy class. Some sites organized classes by the English proficiency levels of the students rather than by grade level. Other sites were designated as ninth-grade schools, where high-school-age students with 8 or fewer years of

FIGURE **2.3** ■

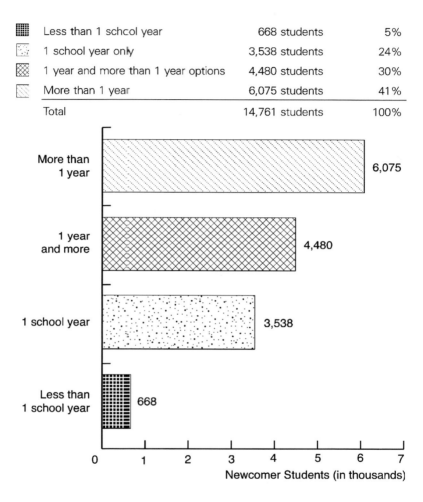

	Less than 1 school year	668 students	5%
	1 school year only	3,538 students	24%
	1 year and more than 1 year options	4,480 students	30%
	More than 1 year	6,075 students	41%
	Total	14,761 students	100%

Number of Students in Programs of Various Lengths

schooling enrolled for 1 year, then moved on to 10th grade in one of the other district high schools.

Type of Language Program

Newcomer programs designate themselves as ESL, bilingual, or native language literacy programs. An ESL program generally provides English language development courses and content area courses in English using special sheltered strategies to make the content comprehensible (see Echevarria, Vogt, & Short, 2004). Bilingual programs generally offer content area courses in both English and the native language of the students. Obviously this is possible only when a large percentage of the students speak the same native language. Native language literacy programs generally provide a number of courses in the students' native language for those who lack literacy skills in any language or whose native language skills are below grade level.

The choice of approach depends on the students' native languages and the availability of bilingual teachers, paraprofessionals, and instructional materials. In 1999-2000, 50% of the programs defined themselves as ESL programs, 7% as bilingual programs, and 2% as native language literacy programs. The remaining 41% combined these program types, offering bilingual, ESL, and native language literacy courses to match the needs of the students.

Some newcomer programs offer both ESL and bilingual options (e.g., content courses taught through Spanish for Spanish speakers and sheltered content taught through English for speakers of other languages). Other programs distinguish between nonliterate and literate students. Literate students may have one set of courses available to them and remain in the program for 1 year, while nonliterate students have additional literacy courses and may remain in the program for a longer time.

Overall, 33% of the programs offered a bilingual program option, 35% offered a native language literacy option, and 90% offered an ESL option. All 115 programs offered English language courses.

Identification and Placement of Students

An important aspect of newcomer programs in all districts is the assessment of incoming students to determine their eligibility for the program. Thirty-six percent of the newcomer programs rely on district intake centers to assess and place students. In the other 64%, teachers or committees within the schools identify and place newcomers. All the programs allow student entry at midterm or midyear.

The majority of newcomer programs (about 87%) accept all students who are eligible for newcomer services. In a few districts (about 7%), not all newcomer students can be served due to limited resources. In some cases, students are placed on a waiting list and enter regular ESL or bilingual programs until space becomes available in the newcomer program. Some students who are eligible for the newcomer program may choose instead to enter language support programs (ESL, bilingual, native language), or an older learner may choose to enter an adult ESL or GED program.

Assessments used for identification and placement are described later in this chapter. In addition to placement tests, staff consider transcripts and report cards students may bring with them from their home country, writing samples, oral interviews with students and parents, and home language surveys to determine appropriate educational placements.

Exit Criteria and Maximum Length of Stay

Most newcomer programs assess students' readiness to make the transition out of the program according to specific exit criteria. The exception to this is the 4-year high school model, in which students fulfill graduation requirements to complete the program. Forty-two percent of the programs use test scores to determine a student's readiness to exit the program, while 34% require a teacher recommendation. Other exit criteria that are frequently considered include evaluation of the student's progress, usually by program staff and portfolio assessment. In most programs, students exit whenever they achieve the exit criteria. In 39% of the programs, students exit when they have completed the specified length of time of the program.

The maximum length of stay in a newcomer program varies from one semester or less in 4% of the programs to more than eight semesters in 7% of the programs (primarily those that are 4-year high schools). Although the maximum stay for over half of the programs (54%) is two to three semesters, the average stay is one to two semesters in 69% of the programs.

Class Size

Although class size in the 115 newcomer programs varies greatly across programs, it is worth noting that many of the programs have smaller class sizes for newcomer students than for other students. Four percent of the programs average fewer than 10 students per class. Nearly half of the programs (49%) serve between 10 and 19 students per class, 25% of the programs serve between 20 and 24 students per class, and 22% serve between 25 and 35 students per class. One factor that influences class size is the total number of students in the newcomer program. For example, 10 of the programs with a class size of 25-35 students are large programs that serve more than 200 students.

Additional factors that influence class size are available resources, funding, and the type of class. For example, enrollment in a native language literacy class may be lower than in a sheltered content class in the same program because not all newcomer students require literacy skill development. Keeping classes small maximizes the amount of time that teachers and paraprofessionals can reasonably spend with individual students and small groups. Some programs limit class size to a specific number, and when students entering at midterm increase the class size beyond the specified limit, additional classes are created and more staff are hired.

Funding Sources

Newcomer programs often utilize multiple sources to fund their operating expenses. Eighty-two percent of the programs receive local school district funds, 52% receive state funds, and 53% receive federal funds. Most programs rely on a combination of funding from these sources;

23% of the programs receive funding from all three sources. Only 5% of the programs rely solely on federal funds, 4% solely on state funds, and 26% solely on district funds. A few programs receive funding from private sources or tuition payments. The most effective and sustained programs seem to be those that receive strong support and the major share of their funding from the local school district.

Instructional Design and Assessment

As mentioned previously, newcomer programs are generally designed to provide intensive, specialized instruction for a limited period of time and offer courses that are distinct from those of the district's regular language support program. For example, they may offer a course to facilitate students' social and cultural integration into American life by familiarizing the students with their community, school routines, and educational expectations. Many programs supplement classroom curricula with field trips, cultural activities, and special events that facilitate the achievement of these acculturation goals. The programs are also concerned with students' academic development and may develop special courses to accommodate gaps in the students' formal education or to accelerate their learning, such as condensing 2 years' worth of middle school science into 1 year.

English Language and Literacy Development

Although they are beyond the expected age (by U.S. standards) of initial literacy instruction, many newcomer students become literate for the first time in their newcomer programs, in their first language or in English. Table 2.2 (page 34) shows some of the prevailing types of instruction provided by the programs. All of the 115 newcomer programs offer English as a second language or English language development (ELD) courses. Over 40% of the programs have courses to develop the students' native language literacy skills. Ninety-seven percent provide some content instruction through English or the native language of the students.

TABLE **2.2** ■

Type of Instruction	Number of Programs	Percent of Programs
English Language Courses	115	100%
Native Language Literacy	48	42%
Content Instruction	112	97%
via Sheltered Instruction (SI)	102	89%
via Native Language Instruction (NLI)	63	55%
via both SI and NLI	53	46%
Cross-Cultural/Orientation to the U.S.	93	81%

Type of Instruction in Programs

Instructors use a wide variety of strategies and techniques to help students develop their native language and English literacy skills. Many programs reported using sheltered instruction techniques such as small cooperative learning groups, scaffolding, modeling, hands-on activities, visual aids, graphic organizers, and realia; they also provide native language support when possible. The programs incorporated computer programs for reading and writing; basic reading strategies (e.g., phonics instruction) with low-level, high-interest selections; instruction in the writing process; oral skills through conversation, role plays, drama, and presentations; the whole language approach; and the language experience approach to teach literacy. Students in many programs were taught language learning strategies and study skill techniques to enhance their English acquisition.

Content Area Courses

Of the 115 programs profiled in 1999-2000, 97% provided instruction in one or more core content areas and in some elective areas, through English or the native language of the students. The course options depended on the length of the daily program, student needs, and the availability of qualified staff and materials. As Table 2.2 reveals, content instruction was delivered through different instructional approaches. Sheltered instruction and bilingual content instruction were implemented to promote the development of core academic skills and knowledge. Sheltered instruction also furthers students' English language development. Over half of the programs (55%) taught content through the native language of the students. Eighty-nine percent taught content through sheltered instruction, which is delivered primarily in English, but the content is made comprehensible through specialized strategies and techniques (see Echevarria, Vogt, & Short, 2004).

Math is the most common offering among programs that offer content instruction. Math is taught in 79% of the programs, followed by language arts in 70%, social studies in 70%, and science in 66%. More than 80% of the programs provide newcomer students with cross-cultural information and orientation to the United States.

Some programs offer additional sheltered or native language content courses such as accounting, art, citizenship, computer technology, dance, economics, music, physical education, social skills, and speech. Students in the 4-year newcomer high schools are provided with all of the courses required for graduation in the regular district high school(s). In newcomer programs of shorter duration, some courses in the regular school program are available to students while they are enrolled in the newcomer programs, particularly in the program-within-a-school model.

Languages of Instruction

Programs were more likely to teach content via the students' native languages when they had a large number of students from the same language background and access to appropriate teachers and instructional materials. Seventy-five percent of the programs reported using a language other than English for some content instruction—either as a subject taught primarily through the native language or as native language support in a sheltered content class—or for native language literacy classes. In many programs, bilingual paraprofessionals provided the native language assistance.

Programs reported a total of 24 native languages used for instruction: Albanian, Amharic, Arabic, Bengali, Bosnian, Cambodian, Cantonese, Dinka (Sudanese), French Creole, Haitian Creole, Hmong, Japanese, Korean, Lao, Mandarin, Nuer, Polish, Russian, Serbo-Croatian, Somali, Spanish, Tagalog, Tigrinya, and Vietnamese.

The most common language used for native language instruction was Spanish (70%), with Vietnamese a distant second at 9%. Languages used less frequently (in four to eight programs) were Arabic, Cantonese, Haitian Creole, Lao, Mandarin, Russian, and Somali. The remaining languages were used in one to three programs.

Career Orientation

Forty-two percent of the programs offered career awareness courses, and 55%, primarily at the high school level, provided career counseling. Some programs offered vocational education or work internships so that students could develop practical skills and knowledge about job opportunities. This training was very useful for students who were not inclined toward postsecondary academic options or who were over age and did not have time to finish high school before reaching the maximum school age. In some instances, work internships utilized students' native language skills as a resource.

Instructional Supports

Some programs offered additional support systems to promote the students' acquisition of language and content knowledge. Seventy-seven percent of the programs, for example, offered study skills development to newcomer students. Seventy-three percent offered tutoring. Forty-three percent of the programs participated in Title I, and 54% provided special education services for referred students. However, only 22% of the programs offered gifted and talented education services. This is an area of concern for several programs, and they have looked for ways to enrich the curriculum for identified gifted students.

Credit for High School Courses

Recognizing the limited time that high-school-aged newcomer students have in school before graduation, a number of programs have implemented courses for which the students may receive credit applicable toward a diploma. Thirty-two of the 53 high school programs (60%) reported that they offer credit for some newcomer classes. The classes that most frequently receive credit are math (43%) and ESL (34%). Other courses that are offered for credit include art, computers, health, language arts (English and Spanish), physical education, science, and social studies. In keeping with state requirements, most core courses taken for credit were staffed by certified content area instructors.

Student Assessment

Programs expressed concern about finding assessments that were appropriate for evaluating newcomer students' knowledge bases in English, the native language, and academic subject areas. To date, no program has reported finding a single assessment that meets their needs, so they rely on a combination of measures to provide a more complete picture than one test alone can provide. Both norm-referenced and criterion-referenced assessments are used across newcomer programs to determine the initial placement of students or their readiness to exit the program, or to measure their progress or achievement. About 80% of the programs use commercially produced assessments to measure students' English language skills, and about half use such assessments to measure students' native language skills.

Across programs, the most commonly used assessment instruments are the *Language Assessment Scales (LAS),* used by 29% of the programs; the *IDEA Proficiency Tests (IPT),* used by 23%; the *Language Assessment Battery (LAB),* used by 17%; and the *Woodcock-Muñoz Language Survey,* used by 14%. These tests measure English or Spanish language proficiency to determine initial placement and to measure progress in the program. Other commercially produced tests that are used include *Aprenda, Bilingual Syntax Measure (BSM), Maculaitis, Stanford Achievement Test (SAT 9), Secondary Level English Proficiency (SLEP), Spanish Assessment of Basic Education (SABE),* and *Texas Assessment of Academic Skills (TAAS).*

Some districts have developed their own assessment instruments to measure language proficiency and achievement in the content areas. Sixty percent of the programs assess students' math skills in English, 30% assessed students' knowledge of science, and 31% assessed their knowledge of social studies. A number of programs assessed students in the core content areas through their native languages: 31% in math, 12% in science, and 15% in social studies.

Classroom-based assessments used in newcomer programs are similar to those found in other school programs. Multiple measures such as writing samples, quizzes, performance assessments, teacher-recorded checklists of student behaviors and skills, participation in oral group activities, homework, and class projects are typically used to assess student language and content growth. Alternative assessments such as portfolios are also used. Most programs use a combination of commercially produced tests and alternative assessments for the various purposes mentioned above.

Table 2.3 shows the 10 most frequently used assessments for placement in the secondary school newcomer programs, as well as the languages in which the students are tested. Where two languages are listed for one assessment instrument, some programs use the instrument in both languages, but this is not always the case. The five formal assessments that are used most widely for exit criteria are the *LAS,* the *IPT,* the *LAB,* the *Woodcock-Muñoz Language Survey,* and the *SOLOM.*

TABLE **2.3**■

Assessment Instruments	Languages	Number of Programs	Percentage of Programs
LAS (Language Assessment Scales)	English	33	29%
	Spanish	14	12%
IPT (IDEA Proficiency Tests)	English	26	23%
	Spanish	7	6%
LAB (Language Assessment Battery)	English	20	17%
	Spanish	8	7%
Woodcock Muñoz Language Survey	English	15	13%
	Spanish	6	5%
SOLOM	English	6	5%
(Student Oral Language Observation Matrix)	Other Lgs	3	3%
TAAS (Texas Assessment of Academic Skills)	English	8	7%
Aprenda	Spanish	7	6%
Maculaitis	English	7	6%
SAT 9	English	6	5%
(Stanford Achievement Tests, 9th ed.)			
SLEP (Secondary Level English Proficiency)	English	6	5%

Most Frequently Used Assessments for Placement

Staffing and Professional Development

Staffing in newcomer programs often includes an administrator, teachers, guidance counselors, and paraprofessionals. A goal of many programs is to hire staff who speak the native languages of the students. All of the 115 programs in our database reported at least one staff member who was proficient in one of the students' native languages. Seventy-eight percent of the programs reported 1 to 10 staff members who were proficient in at least one of the native languages in the program, and a few programs (4%) reported as many as 30 such staff members. Bilingual support staff who are familiar with the students' first languages and cultures are particularly valuable. Newcomer programs need to have staff who can interact with parents and who understand the cultural background of the students' families. Such staff can communicate the schools' expectations for parent involvement in the education of their children (Mace-Matluck, Alexander-Kasparik, & Queen, 1998; Te, 1997).

Administration

Ninety-seven percent of the newcomer programs had administrators. In 28%, the administrators had full-time appointments; in 69%, their appointment to the newcomer program was part-time. Seventy-two percent of the programs had a single administrator. Twenty-four percent had from two to five administrators, depending on the number of students served or on the number of sites in the program. Approximately 4% of the newcomer programs reported no administrator.

Teaching Staff

Many newcomer programs are selective in the recruitment of their instructional personnel, looking for teachers and paraprofessionals experienced in working with recent immigrants in literacy, bilingual, or sheltered instruction classes. Newcomer programs also seek teachers who have had training in second language acquisition theory, ESL and sheltered instruction methods, and cross-cultural communication. The number of teachers per program ranges from 1 to 76. Clearly, this number is a function of the number of students served. Approximately half

(57%) of the programs have two to seven teachers, and 18% employ 16 to 39 teachers. Twenty percent of the programs reported from one to six resource teachers in addition to the regular teaching staff. Resource teachers' positions included ESL coordinator, Title VII (now known as Title III) coordinator, bilingual specialist, and curriculum development specialist.

Ninety-six percent of the programs have certified ESL teachers, 55% have certified bilingual teachers, and 83% have teachers certified in one or more of the content areas. All of the programs have either certified ESL teachers or certified bilingual teachers or both. Having teachers certified in the content areas is particularly important for high school programs that want to offer graduation credit for some courses.

Paraprofessional Support
Bilingual paraprofessionals play important roles in most newcomer programs. In 63% of the programs, bilingual paraprofessionals work full time; in 30%, they work part time. Across programs, the bilingual paraprofessionals speak a total of 40 languages. Twenty-three percent of the programs employ monolingual paraprofessionals as well. The majority of these monolingual aides speak English, but others speak French, Polish, or Russian. Most of the monolingual aides are employed full time.

Eighty-three percent of the programs employ from 1 to 19 bilingual paraprofessionals to assist students in academic domains and native language/literacy development and to facilitate links between the school and the students' families. In most of the bilingual programs, certified bilingual teachers deliver content instruction in the native language, sometimes with support from bilingual aides. In non-bilingual programs, bilingual aides provide support or clarification in the native language in the context of English-medium classes. They may also provide some content instruction or tutoring, as well as input for assessment purposes.

Bilingual paraprofessionals make connections with the newcomer students' families and often provide supplemental guidance and counseling. For example, some students' families have low literacy skills in their native language. Bilingual paraprofessionals can communicate with these families orally to mediate the literacy barriers and assist in meeting student or family needs.

Guidance Counselors

Eighty-nine percent of the programs provide students with access to guidance counselors. Although some of the larger programs employ their own guidance counselors, newcomer students in many schools are served by the regular counselors. Most of the whole-school and separate-school programs have more than one counselor: Whole-school programs have from one to six counselors; separate-school programs have from one to four. Sixty-eight percent of the programs have bilingual counselors. Across these programs, counselors speak a total of more than 15 languages.

Professional Development

Eighty-four percent of the programs reported that they provide specific staff training related to newcomer issues. In 28% of the programs, all school staff are invited to participate. Thirty-nine percent invite newcomer staff and other language support staff (i.e., ESL, sheltered, and/or bilingual teachers and paraprofessionals). In 20% of the programs, only teachers participate. Some programs provide newcomer staff development not only for the teachers in the program, but also for those who receive students after they leave the newcomer program, so they will be better prepared to meet the students' cognitive, linguistic, academic, and emotional needs.

Across programs, these are the most frequently addressed topics during staff development meetings: assessment, student behavior and classroom management, cross-cultural issues (e.g., home country schooling practices, family interaction patterns, cultural norms of behavior), curriculum development, instructional methodologies, the use of technology, literacy development, materials preparation, newcomer families, orientation to and transition out of the program, school issues, scheduling, and staff issues. Other topics arise on a case-by-case basis. District personnel, program staff, or faculty from local and state universities provide most of the professional development. Approximately 38% of the programs reported monthly or ongoing professional development opportunities.

Transition Measures

Effective programs have an articulated plan for moving students through the language development and content courses offered in the newcomer program and into a regular program (ESL, bilingual, or mainstream). This articulation includes a sequenced curriculum for English language acquisition as well as a series of courses to help students either further their content knowledge or to address gaps in their educational backgrounds. Some programs are designed to promote the students' native language skills, too, and link to other courses upon exit from the newcomer program. For example, students may take a pre-algebra class in the newcomer program to prepare them for a mainstream algebra class after they leave.

Students automatically exit from many of the 1-year programs when the school year ends. A number of programs test students for language proficiency (and some test content areas as well) to determine whether the newcomers are ready to participate in the other school programs. However, most programs allow some degree of flexibility. Some students who make fast progress can exit before the end of the program term. Students who arrive in the second semester of the year, have large gaps in their educational backgrounds, or haven't acquired literacy skills, may receive an extension of their time in the program.

The majority of newcomer programs place exiting students into a program of instruction that includes one or a combination of the following: ESL, bilingual, native language literacy, sheltered, or mainstream courses, according to the student's specific needs and the options available in the district. The data reveal that there is no standard practice for facilitating the transition of students out of the newcomer program and into another language support or regular academic program. In fact, transition procedures have not always been articulated in a newcomer program design and, in some instances, were not considered until the first set of students was ready to exit.

Transition Process for Students in Home Schools

The majority of the newcomer programs last for 1 year and are located within a larger school. Consequently, for most of the students in these programs, the transition is relatively uncomplicated because they are already in their home schools. Similarly, students who attend newcomer classes at a separate site for a half day are at their home schools for the other part of the day, so their transition is easier than for students who are at a separate site for a full day. Some students who are at programs within a school or at half-day separate sites may take a mainstream math or elective course (e.g., art, cooking, music, physical education, typing) while still enrolled in the newcomer program to facilitate their integration with students in mainstream classes.

In a few schools, students are given the opportunity to observe ESL, sheltered, and mainstream content classes before entering the regular ESL program. In other programs, students are encouraged to audit a course outside the newcomer program before exiting. Under this plan, a student may join a class on a temporary basis, after which the student and teacher decide if it is an appropriate placement. In some programs, students exit from the program one course at a time, so they make the transition gradually to regular ESL and content classes according to their individual abilities. For example, a student may take a regular math class and a newcomer social studies class during the same term.

In a number of programs, the teachers who provide instruction for the newcomers also teach in the regular ESL program, which helps smooth the transition process. Some newcomer center teachers and regular ESL teachers have shared planning time and interact daily to review students' progress. Content teachers who teach newcomer students often work with bilingual aides who provide native language support and other assistance as needed.

The integration of newcomer students with mainstream students is enhanced when students in newcomer classes collaborate with students in mainstream classes on special projects for the school or community. These programs also encourage the newcomers to participate with the full student body in extracurricular activities such as athletic events, multicultural assemblies, field trips, dances, and career field experiences.

Transition to Home School

Many newcomer programs serve students from more than one home school. When these students leave the programs to return to their home schools, the newcomer staff offer a number of measures to assist them in making the transition. Thirty-seven percent of the programs arrange for orientation, pre-registration activities, and visitation to regular middle schools or high schools. For most students who make the transition to other schools, counselors help facilitate their move by planning the visits to the home school or, when options are available, assisting the students in choosing a school that would be appropriate for their needs and interests. Some counselors at newcomer centers continue to monitor the students' progress and adjustment for a time after they have made the transition to the home school, but this practice is not common.

In other programs, a newcomer teacher takes the lead in organizing the transition process. Parents and the newcomer students may also be actively involved in making these arrangements. In some programs, parents are required to submit a request that their child transfer to the attendance area school rather than remaining in the school that houses the newcomer and ESL programs. If a newcomer program does not organize a formal visitation, the staff may encourage parents and students to visit the home school on their own prior to enrolling there.

In one school, a committee consisting of the home school ESL teacher, newcomer center staff, parents, and the student develop an individualized plan for the transition. At another school, newcomer students attend a culmination ceremony at the end of their program to receive honors, scholarships, certificates, and trophies. This helps the students recognize their accomplishments and prepare for the next phase of their education. A number of schools use a pen pal or buddy system to pair newcomer students with more advanced ESL students (preferably from the same language background) in the home school to assist them in adjusting to the new environment. In some districts, tutorials, meetings, or mentoring with teachers in the home schools are provided during the first semester after the transition.

Some newcomer programs are modeled after the regular ESL program. Their curricula may be similar to the regular schools' curricula, and they have a school day and individual classes that are structured similarly to those of the schools in the area. Consequently, when the students enter regular programs in their home schools, they have an understanding of the structure of the school day and the expectations of the programs.

Students who attend the ninth- and tenth-grade newcomer high schools may attend a high school fair that provides them with information about the numerous options available to them. Some students may choose a high school program linked with a university, vocational, or work-study program. A school-to-work transition program within the schools and higher education counseling educate newcomer students and their families about opportunities in the United States. Some newcomer students do not finish high school because they are older than typical high school students in the United States, but they go on to find jobs after leaving the program.

In some cases, students graduate directly from newcomer schools that offer a 4-year high school program. The seven newcomer programs that provide a full high school education give students an orientation to the school when they enroll. Most students remain in these high schools until they graduate. However, if a student decides to transfer to a regular high school program, newcomer staff facilitate the transition in several ways, such as introducing the student to a counselor and an ESL teacher at the high school to which the student is transferring and completing the necessary paperwork. At one school, newcomer staff adjust the schedule and provide transportation so that a transferring student may take a mainstream content class or a half-day mainstream program in the other school for a trial period before completing the transition.

Parent and Community Connections

Most newcomer programs offer their students additional services beyond English language and academic courses. Sixty-seven percent of the programs offer physical health services, 42% offer mental health services, and 43% offer social services. These may be on-site services or referrals. A few of the programs provide child care or legal referrals. Thirty-five percent of the programs engage in community outreach, and 24% have partnerships with the community linked to local and national government organizations, universities, community and national youth organizations, athletic groups, health organizations, libraries, businesses, cultural and church organizations, charities, or social services.

Most newcomer programs seek to include the whole family in the life of the school. They arrange family events and provide activities that will acclimate the newcomer parents to the school and community. They also help families connect with appropriate social and health services, as needed. Seventy percent of the programs conduct active parental outreach. To support these efforts, 62% have a school liaison who works with parents. Sixty-six percent of the programs have adult ESL classes available either at the program site or at another district location, and 36% make adult basic education classes available. Twenty-four percent offer native language literacy classes for adults. Forty-eight percent of the programs provide orientation for parents to U.S. schools, and 43% provide orientation to the United States.

Many other services are offered to students or their families in specific newcomer programs. These services include access to educational organizations that provide the following:

- Counseling on topics such as post-traumatic stress disorder and substance abuse prevention
- Migrant education
- Computer or technology training
- Mentoring and tutoring programs before and after school
- Afterschool clubs
- Evening literacy classes
- Afterschool ESL classes (for students and parents)
- Saturday school
- Test preparation
- Arts programs
- Parenting programs
- Internships in conjunction with career education and work programs

Services targeted specifically for parents include

- Translation and interpretation services
- Newsletters in various languages
- GED courses in Spanish
- Citizenship classes
- Employment services

Summary

This chapter reveals the wide variation among newcomer programs and demonstrates the range of features a program might incorporate into its design. The features described were based on the categories in the CREDE research survey questionnaire. There may be additional characteristics of the programs that did not come to light and that might only be revealed through site visits and in-depth interviews—although we did ask for additional comments on each questionnaire to help us understand each program as fully as possible.

Many programs told us during the research study that their programs evolved over time. They field tested some ideas for the program, such as staffing or scheduling or transition procedures, then determined which aspects of the programs to keep and which to change. The programs also advised that significant changes in the student population or the educational climate might necessitate course and staffing changes.

When Township High School District 214 established its newcomer program, one priority was to design a curriculum that
would provide students with access to technology for their
academic learning.

Establishing an Effective Newcomer Program

This study has been a resource for newcomer program teachers and directors and schools who would like to start [a newcomer program]. It has given light to the need for programs to assist newcomers. I have had people come to observe our program to carry ideas to their own schools.

—Jane Long Middle School, Houston Texas

Developing a newcomer program needs to be a thoughtful, informed, and iterative process. It involves reaching out to a variety of stakeholder groups, conducting research on program design options, visiting existing programs, seeking funding sources not only for staffing the program but also for transporting students and obtaining specialized resources, and pulling together all the information into a program design that fits the goals of the district and the needs of the students. Many of the programs we studied were created independently as districts perceived a need and developed an intervention to address it. These programs lacked knowledge of other program models, or knew of only one or two, and so may have been limited in their conception of program design options. This book and our online database can help districts considering a newcomer program learn about the options available to them and about existing programs they can visit.

We have noted that close to 75% of the secondary newcomer programs in our database were established in the past decade. It is reasonable to assume that more districts will consider this programmatic option for their students. As they begin their research, they will find that there are common features across all newcomer programs but that many choices and decisions still need to be made when establishing a new program. This chapter describes the initial steps a district might take when considering a newcomer program option, then explains the later phases of planning and implementation. Specific details from the case of a recently developed program, the Newcomer Center in Arlington Heights, Illinois, conclude the chapter.

Common Features of Newcomer Programs

Although there is a great deal of variability in the design and implementation of a newcomer program, all programs have the following common features. These should be kept in mind when initial discussions about setting up a newcomer program take place and accounted for as program development unfolds.

- *A cohort of newcomer students.* A newcomer program must have a sufficient number of new immigrant students whose needs are not being met in the regular ESL or bilingual language programs.
- *A program or set of courses distinct from the regular language support program.* The newcomer program is generally designed to provide intensive, specialized instruction for a limited period of time. Upon exit from the program, students may enter a regular ESL, bilingual, or mainstream education program.
- *A plan for English as a second language development.* All newcomer programs have ESL courses or English language development courses that may be the equivalent of a sheltered language arts class. A specified period of time is devoted each school day to promoting the students' English acquisition.
- *Instructional strategies for literacy development.* Many newcomer students become literate for the first time in these programs, in their first language and/or English. These programs develop the students' academic literacy skills.

- *Instructional strategies for the integration of language and content.* Sheltered and bilingual content instruction is planned to help students acquire core content knowledge while furthering their language skills. Eighty-nine percent of the programs offer at least one core content course through a sheltered instruction approach.
- *Courses or activities for student orientation to U.S. schools and the community.* Newcomer programs pay particular attention to familiarizing students with school routines and educational expectations in the United States, with American culture, and with the community and the United States. Many of the programs supplement classroom curricula with field trips, cultural activities, and special events.
- *Experienced teachers.* Many newcomer programs hand-pick their staff, looking for teachers and paraprofessionals experienced in working with recent immigrants in literacy, bilingual, or sheltered classes. Staff who are bilingual and represent the languages and cultures of the students add value to the program.
- *Appropriate materials, especially for students with no to low literacy and limited formal schooling.* Instructional materials must be cognitively appropriate for the students' age with linguistic modifications. Content materials should be selected to help students learn the foundations of subjects they may not have studied or to further develop their prior content knowledge. It is also important for students to have access to literature selections in English and their native languages.
- *Paraprofessional support.* Almost all of the programs utilize paraprofessional support, especially bilingual staff, to help students in content classes and native language literacy courses and to facilitate communication with the students' families.
- *Family connections.* Most newcomer programs express the importance of welcoming the whole family to the school and arrange family events, adult ESL classes, and other activities for them. They also help families link to social and health services.

Features to Address When Establishing a Newcomer Program

The Checklist for Establishing a Newcomer Program (see below) is a useful tool for planning purposes. In addition to addressing the common program features described above, districts must make many decisions about the features of their program in order to implement an effective model that serves the distinct needs of their newcomer population. The checklist is organized into three areas that should be addressed sequentially: 1) exploration, 2) planning, and 3) implementation. However, not all items within each section need to proceed in order; some of the items can be decided independently, whereas others can be determined only after a series of decisions are made. Following the checklist, we provide a more detailed explanation of each item.

Checklist for Establishing a Newcomer Program

Exploration

_____ **Leadership:** Form a leadership team, convey the vision of the program, meet with stakeholder groups, and commit to seeing the process through.

_____ **Newcomer definition:** Define the criteria that will be used to identify newcomer students.

_____ **Student population:** Determine if there are enough students to constitute a program and decide how many students to serve.

_____ **Goal setting:** Set realistic student learning goals for language and content knowledge and programmatic goals.

_____ **Program design:** Identify the grade levels to be served and the potential program design.

_____ **Language(s) of instruction:** Select the languages to be used in instruction and the types of classes in which they will be used (e.g., ESL, bilingual, native language literacy, academic content).

___ **Administrative approval:** Meet with the district administration and seek approval to continue the exploration process.

___ **Location:** Find a site to house the newcomer program.

___ **Funding:** Identify sources of funds for program development and implementation.

___ **Program site visits:** Visit well-established newcomer programs, especially those close in design to the anticipated program design.

Planning

___ **School board approval:** Meet with and gain support from the local school board.

___ **District level coordination:** Coordinate with other educational programs in the district to ensure access to appropriate services and articulation with other programs.

___ **Stakeholder input:** Gather input from stakeholder groups regarding program design.

___ **Program director:** Designate a part-time or full-time administrator for the program.

___ **Program design:** Finalize the program design based on input, target population, location options, and funding.

___ **Grade levels:** Determine which grade levels will be served and how students will be organized within the program.

___ **Course offerings:** Select the courses to offer based on program goals, staff, resources, daily length of program, student background, and so on.

_____ **Scheduling:** Establish a daily schedule for the program courses.

_____ **Curriculum:** Find or develop curricula for the newcomer courses.

_____ **Materials:** Select or develop instructional resources that are appropriate for the age and cognitive level of the students.

_____ **Internships:** Set up work internships or career awareness opportunities for secondary school students.

_____ **Transportation:** As needed to serve the target population, organize transportation to bring students to the newcomer program site.

_____ **Extended time for learning:** Where possible, identify extended time for student learning, such as afterschool, summer, or intersession opportunities.

_____ **Placement policies:** Determine where students will be assessed for initial identification and placement and what placement options will be available.

_____ **Assessment:** Determine which assessments will be used with newcomer students and for which purposes.

_____ **Transition strategies:** Plan transition procedures for students who will exit the program and ensure course articulation between the newcomer program and the receiving program.

_____ **Student monitoring:** Develop a plan for monitoring students' progress after they leave the newcomer program, and use that data for program improvement.

____ **Program evaluation:** Plan a formative evaluation that includes collection and analysis of student data.

____ **Baseline data collection:** Document the current educational conditions in terms of course offerings, newcomer student achievement, staff preparation, and so on before implementing a newcomer program.

Implementation

____ **Student recruitment:** Through school and community networks, recruit students for the first year of the program's operation.

____ **Staffing:** Recruit and hire experienced teachers with knowledge of literacy development and sheltered content instructional approaches.

____ **Paraprofessionals:** Recruit and train paraprofessionals with language and cultural backgrounds similar to those of the newcomer students.

____ **Guidance counselors:** Identify and train guidance staff to work with newcomer students.

____ **Translators and interpreters:** Identify and recruit staff and on-call translators and interpreters.

____ **Staff development:** Establish and implement an ongoing professional development plan for newcomer program staff.

____ **Student orientation:** Carry out activities that support student orientation to the educational system and the community.

____ **Integration with native English speakers:** Implement meaningful activities whereby English-speaking students and newcomer students interact.

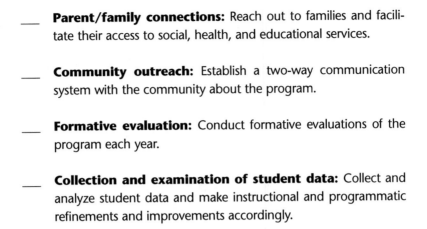

___ **Parent/family connections:** Reach out to families and facilitate their access to social, health, and educational services.

___ **Community outreach:** Establish a two-way communication system with the community about the program.

___ **Formative evaluation:** Conduct formative evaluations of the program each year.

___ **Collection and examination of student data:** Collect and analyze student data and make instructional and programmatic refinements and improvements accordingly.

Exploration

Leadership

The first step is to form a leadership team to develop and convey the vision and mission of the newcomer program. Often this process begins with one or two dedicated staff members who notice that some English language learners are not succeeding in school, even in designated language support programs such as the ESL or bilingual program. This person or these persons conduct the initial research on newcomer centers then enlist others to support the design and implementation. Having several people involved as part of the leadership team is recommended for division of labor and for long-term commitment to the program.

Newcomer definition/Student population

After the leaders articulate a vision for a newcomer program, the next step is to determine if there is an appropriate student population. For a newcomer program to be feasible, it must have a sufficient number of new immigrant students whose needs are not being met in the regular ESL or bilingual language programs. In order to facilitate the identification process, the program developers must define a newcomer student and establish criteria for the definition, such as length of time in the United States, age, educational background, native language, and so on. Using the definition, a district can determine how many newcomer students are present and consider how many to serve in the new program.

Goal setting

The next major step is to set goals for the program. These goals should include student learning objectives for language (English and perhaps the native language to promote bilingualism) and for content (organized by subject area) and should be realistic given the daily schedule and expected time that students will remain in the program. For example, a half-day program for 1 year cannot substantively teach ESL, mathematics, U.S. history, life science, Spanish language arts, and health to the participating students. Programmatic goals may be set as well, such as increasing the number of students served over several years, creating school-community partnerships, integrating newcomer and English-speaking students in meaningful ways, and so on.

Program design

At this point, the developers are ready to identify the potential program design. They need to estimate how many students to serve, which grade levels to include, whether to operate a full- or half-day program, how long to have students remain in the program, whether to create a program within a school or at a separate site, and which courses to offer. To help them decide on these matters, they may study how existing newcomer programs operate. Early design ideas are likely to be modified over time, with the final design emerging only as new information—about possible locations, funding, and staffing, for example—becomes known.

Language(s) of instruction

The next step is to decide the language(s) of instruction. The choice of languages has implications for staffing, curriculum development, and instructional resources. As discussed in chapter 2, 89% of the programs provide some content instruction in English; approximately 62% provide some instruction in the native language of the students, usually Spanish. Many programs begin as a bilingual or ESL program. Larger and more experienced programs may provide options that they have developed over time to meet the needs of their student body. Examples from three programs follow:

- Most classes are taught in English but Spanish language arts is available for one period each day for native Spanish speakers.
- Spanish- and Mandarin-speaking students have science instruction in their native language while all other newcomers have sheltered science.
- All courses are taught through English using the sheltered instruction approach, but native language paraprofessionals are present in content classes to clarify information and assist the students.

Administrative approval

At this point, it is important to begin sharing ideas and information with the central administration of the district. Leadership teams often begin with the assistant or deputy superintendent of curriculum and instruction (or someone with a similar function) and set forth their case in favor of establishing a newcomer program. They share their definition of a newcomer student, their data on the lack of success experienced by these students in the regular school programs, their goals for the newcomer program, and their initial ideas about program design. With administration approval, the leadership team can continue these early steps.

Location

Initial discussions about a possible location for the newcomer program should take place next. Most programs try to find locations near the majority of the newcomer students' homes. Thus the program will be centered in the community it is trying to serve, which may reduce transportation costs. Most newcomer programs are designed as programs within a school, where they are articulated with larger ESL or bilingual programs and share resources such as space, staff, and materials. In these settings, many of the services that are offered to mainstream students are available to the newcomer students as well.

Other districts find that a central location in a school or at a separate site is the most effective way to utilize their resources. Students are usually provided with transportation to the central site. Some large urban districts have had difficulty finding sites for the programs due to overcrowded conditions in the schools near the newcomer population. Some districts have converted former warehouses into schools to house a separate-site program. There is also the possibility that a district might want to open several sites. At least 20 districts in our database have more than one newcomer site.

Funding

One key to a successful newcomer program is adequate funding, especially in the start-up years when costs are higher. Given the smaller school or class size, the aim for comprehensive services, the development of special curricula, the greater frequency of field trips to help students learn about their new community and educational resources (e.g., museums), newcomer programs may be more expensive than regular school programs (McDonnell & Hill, 1993). As explained in chapter 2, newcomer programs across the United States regularly use a combination of funding sources to operate their programs, although quite a few began with grants from the U.S. Department of Education. Local, state, and federal funds are often drawn upon; and as programs become more well established, they may turn to private sources, such as business and community sources or charitable foundations, to supplement public funds. At this stage of the process, funding need not be secured, but potential sources of funds should be identified.

Program site visits

The final step in the exploration phase is making program site visits. It is highly recommended that, if possible, the leadership team plus other administration staff visit well-established newcomer programs, especially those similar to the anticipated program design, to see if the operation meshes with their vision and to discuss best practices and barriers to successful implementation. Some professional associations for educators, such as Teachers of English to Teachers of Other Languages

(TESOL) and the National Association for Bilingual Education (NABE), offer school visits during their annual conference, and in the past have included newcomer programs among their school sites. The CAL newcomer directory (www.cal.org/newcomerdb) is another resource for finding appropriate programs to visit.

Planning

School board approval

As program development moves into a more structured planning phase, the local school board must be involved. Getting support from the school board is critical when establishing a program and will likely require a series of meetings with board members to orient them to the needs of the newcomer students and to examine programmatic alternatives. Newcomer programs operate under the same federal, state, and local educational policies as other language support services provided to limited English proficient students in a district.

The local school board will also play a major role in securing funding for the newcomer program. It may be useful to prepare profiles of a range of English language learners in the district, first describing their language and educational backgrounds and their linguistic, schooling, and socialization needs, then identifying the newcomer students within this group to help board members distinguish them and understand their social and academic requirements.

District-level coordination

Coordination at the district level involves discussion among representatives of various instructional and support services so that resources may be shared and articulation planned. It is important to ensure that newcomer students will have access to appropriate services, not only for content and language courses, but also for special education, gifted and talented opportunities, and Title I services. The coordination needs to be ongoing to ensure adequate resource allocation and smooth transitions between the newcomer program and the programs students will move into. The articulation process should include a sequenced curriculum for English language acquisition as well as a series of courses to help students maintain and further their content knowledge or to address gaps in their educational backgrounds.

Stakeholder input

The leadership team will also want to establish communication with various stakeholder groups: other teachers and administrators, parents, community leaders, and so on. Conducting question-and-answer sessions or focus groups with these stakeholders can yield important insights and contributions to the final program design. Principals can share information about what they need to operate their programs more effectively, and this information might be useful in the eventual program design. Sessions for parents could be held in their communities, perhaps at a local recreation center. Meetings with community leaders to gather support for this new initiative help set the foundation for school-community partnerships and career awareness opportunities or possible work internships.

Program director

At this stage, still fairly early in the planning phase, a program director is usually designated, often drawn from the leadership team. Depending on the size of the newcomer population, this administrator may be part-time or full-time. Newcomer program administrators, along with school-level administrators, play a vital role in creating a school climate that accepts diversity as an asset to the school and community. They are responsible for coordinating instruction, providing staff development, and maintaining connections between the newcomer programs and the home schools. They may also assist in securing funding and other support from policy makers and in gathering appropriate data to demonstrate the benefits of the newcomer program.

Program design

Refinement to the initial program design takes place over time. As input from central administrators, school board members, and stakeholders is gathered and reviewed and location and funding options become known, the program design is shaped to the interests, needs, and resources of the school and community. This is an iterative process during which new information and opportunities emerge that may result in design modifications. Depending on the resources available and the students being served, the daily program may involve one or two course periods, half the school day, or the full school day. The length of program enrollment needs to be set in conjunction with program goals, but accommodations may be needed for individual students who need to spend more or less time in the program, depending on their linguistic and academic needs.

Grade levels

Program designers must also determine which grade levels will be served and how students will be organized. Some sites serve all grade levels in the school's category (e.g., Grades 6-8 for middle school programs, Grades 9-12 for high school programs). A number of programs combine middle school and high school students in one location but do not co-mingle the two levels, except perhaps for an initial literacy class. Some sites organize students by English proficiency level rather than by grade level. Other sites are designated, for example, as ninth-grade schools, where high-school-age students with 8 or fewer years of schooling may attend for 1 year, then move on to 10th grade in one of the other district high schools.

Course offerings

The courses that will be offered to the students can be determined more clearly once the design is settled. Depending on the size of the program and resource availability, students may have course options according to their language and educational backgrounds. If possible, high school programs should develop courses for which students can earn credits toward graduation. English language learners often take courses that offer elective credit but may struggle to obtain enough core credits for graduation. If some of the newcomer content courses, such as mathematics, offer core credit, the newcomer students benefit greatly. Titles of these core content courses should be similar to the titles of the courses in the regular education program.

Scheduling

In developing the daily schedule, one recommendation is to parallel existing structures and schedules so students will be acclimated to the regular program when they exit. For example, if the high schools in the district operate on a block schedule, then the newcomer program for high school students would also utilize a block schedule.

Curriculum/Materials/Internships

As the program becomes more refined, the leadership team can begin to select appropriate curricula and materials for the students and courses. In some cases, new curricula may need to be written, such as an accelerated U.S. history course that combines most of the information taught in elementary school into a 1-year program for newcomer students of middle school age. Age-appropriate ESL and bilingual materials for various levels of English and native language proficiency are necessary and may be readily available. However, age-appropriate literacy development materials for older students may be needed but more difficult to find. The newcomer teaching staff frequently develop curricula, assessment measures, and classroom materials tailored to fit their own program and student population.

If the program will serve older learners, especially of high school age, the developers might want to design work internships or vocational education courses that develop some practical skills and knowledge about job opportunities outside of school. This training is very useful for students who are not inclined toward postsecondary academic options or who do not have enough time to finish high school because of age restrictions. The internship planning process is time consuming. Programs that offer work internships, such as the Brooklyn, Manhattan, and Queens International Schools in New York City, continually add new sites to their workplace options and sometimes drop sites. The staff look for at least some workplaces where the students' native language skills will be useful. The program itself usually involves more than just having students go to a work site and carry out specific tasks. Often there are sessions to help orient students to the workplace prior to the start of the internship and weekly school-based meetings to support the internship. These meetings may address concerns the students or workplace staff have about the interaction at work, the workplace culture, expectations of roles and responsibilities, and so on. Placing students with very limited English skills might be a particularly hard challenge, so many programs do not offer work internships in the first semester.

Transportation
Transportation can be a costly aspect of the program, depending on the area served by the newcomer center and the location of the students' homes. Arranging for bus service can be complicated; discussions with the transportation department should begin as soon as the program site is determined. In some programs, students take designated buses to a central location. In other programs, students take the regular school bus to their home school, where the newcomer center is a program within the school.

Extended time for learning
Research shows that providing students with extended time for learning can enhance language acquisition and help students close or narrow significant gaps in their educational backgrounds, so many programs look for opportunities to involve students in clubs, classes, and study sessions beyond the regular school day. When the site is a program within a school, afterschool opportunities are often easier to secure. When the program is at a separate site, the staff often lead extended learning activities themselves or invite parents or others to help after school or on weekends. Transportation needs can be a limiting factor if afterschool buses are unavailable. Extended learning time can also occur on weekends and during the summer. Twenty-three percent of the programs in our database offer summer programs to allow students to continue the learning process during vacation months. Some summer programs are specifically designed for the newcomer students, while others are part of the regular school offerings from the district.

Placement policies

Policies for the identification and placement of newly arrived students should be formalized. Entry criteria must be clearly determined and may include scores below a cutoff level on a battery of assessments such as an English language proficiency test, a native literacy assessment, a test of one or more content areas in English or the native language, a writing assessment, and an oral interview. A review of student transcripts from the native country often occurs as well. Many newcomer programs rely on the district intake center to assess and place the students. If the district does not have a central intake center, a referral process should be set up for students who try to enroll in the district at other schools (those without newcomer programs), particularly after the school year has begun. Once newcomer students have been identified, placement decisions must be made. The options available, such as a basic math or an algebra class, are contingent upon the program design, course offerings, and staffing.

Assessment

Program staff must also identify assessments to use for measuring student growth in language and content knowledge. The goals of the program will influence this process. If, for example, one goal is to develop the students' bilingual abilities, then they must be assessed yearly with language proficiency tests in both English and their native language. Moreover, regulations for programs relying on federal funding require annual assessments in language and key content areas for English language learners.

Some programs, such as the Brooklyn, Manhattan, and Queens International Schools, have used extensive assessment portfolios with their students. Some programs have students take a standardized test, like the Iowa Test of Basic Skills, along with all students in the district, in order to have a baseline measure to track student progress. Certain assessments may also be selected specifically to determine promotion or exit from the program. In general, it is important to identify all the assessments and define their purposes during the planning phase.

Transition strategies

Because the overall goal of newcomer programs is to prepare students for successful entry into the district's regular programs, the transition process is critical. Planning for the transition should not be delayed until students are ready to exit the newcomer program. Rather, exit criteria should be set up in conjunction with the program goals.

There should be ongoing discussions with staff who will receive the former newcomer students, along with activities for the students to acclimate them to their new schools or programs (e.g., school visits, meetings with counselors, extracurricular activities that integrate student groups, classroom observations). This is especially critical for students who attend a newcomer program that is not located at their home school. Planning for the transition is coordinated with other district services, such as transportation, ESL programs, and so forth. In particular, newcomer staff need to be sure that students develop the skills and background knowledge they will need to succeed once they exit the newcomer program.

Student monitoring

Monitoring procedures should be established in order to determine if the students are successful after they leave the newcomer program. Data from this monitoring process can show if the program is meeting its goals and can be used for program improvement. For example, the monitoring process can reveal if newcomer students make the transition to other school programs successfully and are prepared for the literacy and content demands of bilingual, ESL, or mainstream courses. If they are not being successful, the program can be modified accordingly.

Program evaluation

One area where existing newcomer programs have made recent efforts is in program evaluation. Some programs operated for several years without any evaluation process. Others that had Title VII funding evaluated their program and the students while they were enrolled in the program but not after they had exited. It is highly recommended that programs plan a formative evaluation process that examines student language and content development while they are in the program and after they have exited. It is possible to work with the district accountability system to tag the newcomer students and monitor their progress through school. Whether they are in an ESL, bilingual, or mainstream program, collecting and analyzing data on their progress provides valuable information to feed back into the program revision process. Programmatic goals should be evaluated as well, such as acquisition of appropriate literacy and native language materials, completion of a staff development program, development of specialized curricula, and so forth.

Baseline data collection

Collecting baseline data on student achievement prior to implementation of the new program will provide critical information to support subsequent formative and summative evaluations of the program. It is conceivable that several years after the program is established, there will be new staff, administrators, and school board members who are unfamiliar with the achievement levels of newcomer students and other features of the educational environment prior to implementation of the newcomer program. Having relevant data from the years prior to the beginning of the program makes it possible to document program effects in a range of areas such as student achievement, attendance and dropout rates, course offerings, and teacher preparation.

Implementation

Student recruitment

New programs have found that for the first year of operation, they often need to recruit students through school and community networks. Until the newcomer program becomes known in the district and identification and placement procedures have become established, most students are recruited through teacher referrals and community outreach efforts. The communications department of the school district can be a helpful resource in publicizing the newcomer program through press releases, fliers, and brochures. Some programs reported that the existence of a newcomer program in their district attracted newcomer families to the area.

Staffing

Many programs reported the importance of recruiting and hiring experienced teaching staff who are trained to address the special needs of new immigrant students. Specific qualifications can be established. The teachers' background should include an understanding of second language acquisition principles, cross-cultural awareness, sheltered content instruction, and literacy development. If the students represent a diversity of cultures and languages, it is helpful to have staff members who represent the same diversity.

Paraprofessionals

It is often through the hiring of paraprofessionals that newcomer programs achieve a diversity among the staff that parallels the diversity of the students. Eighty-three percent of the programs in the database employ paraprofessionals; most programs have at least some paraprofessionals with language and cultural backgrounds similar to those of the newcomer students. These paraprofessionals often play an important role in helping students who are recent immigrants become acclimated to their new environment. Often the bilingual paraprofessionals are called upon to provide native language support in classrooms where courses are taught in English.

Guidance counselors

Programs with larger numbers of students often hire their own guidance counselors to work specifically with newcomer students. In smaller programs, the regular guidance counselors in the school serve all students, including the newcomers. It is preferable to recruit counselors who are bilingual and who are familiar with the students' cultures and the issues they face. The counselors' responsibilities include assisting the students with adjustment and transition to the new school setting. They may connect students with appropriate social and health services, although some programs have social workers who perform these duties and conduct family outreach as well.

In large districts with many immigrant students, intake centers and guidance counselors cooperate to facilitate placement and transition processes. Ongoing dialogue between newcomer program staff and counselors assures that the counselors are aware of problems that arise so that together they may seek solutions. The counselors need to be in touch with the programs that will receive students upon exit from the newcomer program.

Translators and interpreters

Translation and interpretation are important resources for effective communication with parents and community members and among counselors, students, and other school personnel. To implement the program well, the director or leadership team must identify and recruit translators and interpreters who may be on staff or on call, in paid or volunteer positions.

Staff development

Once the staff have been hired, the program must establish and implement an ongoing staff development plan. Both the teachers in the newcomer program and the teachers who receive the students once they exit the program should participate in staff development programs so they may better serve the students' cognitive, linguistic, academic, and emotional needs. Paraprofessionals should participate in ongoing staff development too.

Student orientation

As the course offerings and curricula are finalized, the program needs to pay attention to student orientation to the school and community. Some programs have developed courses or curriculum units as part of a social studies course specifically for orientation purposes. Other programs plan ongoing field trips and curriculum activities that familiarize students with school routines and expectations, American culture, the community, and the United States. Sometimes these activities include parents as well.

Integration with native English speakers

It is critical for the success of the program to create and implement meaningful opportunities for English-speaking students and newcomer students to interact. Extracurricular clubs and sports provide one means of promoting interaction. Joint activities, such as service learning or community-based projects, offer another approach. Some of the newcomer programs team with the middle and high school foreign language departments to plan events in which both groups of students practice their native and second languages.

Parent and family connections

As described in chapter 1, one of the philosophical goals of newcomer programs is to promote and maintain strong connections with the families of the newcomer students. Once the program has been established, it is important to reach out to families and determine their educational, social, and health needs. With this information, programs can begin to facilitate the family's access to appropriate services. Helping them gain access might involve directing them to existing programs such as district-supported adult ESL and local affordable housing agencies. At other times, the newcomer program or district might undertake new programs to offer, such as family literacy or parenting classes. Community partnerships might bring healthcare professionals to the program site for medical and dental check-ups. As a newcomer program becomes better established, these family and community links can be strengthened and expanded.

Community outreach

While these family connections are being made, outreach to the local community should continue. Information about the program as it opens and grows over time should be shared in the neighborhoods. Opportunities for school and community groups to meet and discuss concerns, suggestions, or emerging needs could become routinized over time. Just as discussions within the school district about the program will be ongoing, conversations with the community representatives should be, too.

Formative evaluation

All successful newcomer programs grow and evolve over time. The formative evaluation process is an important vehicle for improving a program and verifying that it is meeting its goals and student needs. Each year, a formative evaluation of the program's implementation (e.g., curricula, literacy development strategies) and the students' progress should be conducted. The evaluation features may be associated with a funding requirement, but even if they are not, program staff benefit from an analysis of progress toward goals as well as suggestions for improvement.

Collection and examination of student data

A mainstay of a formative evaluation should be the collection and examination of student data. Looking at students' language proficiency and content knowledge growth while in the program and after they have exited provides the most accurate picture of the effectiveness of the program. The evaluation report should be used to make instructional and programmatic refinements. It offers evidence for school policy makers that the newcomer program is beneficial for the students it serves. It may also help convince them to continue funding the program in the event that federal or other funds are no longer available. After several years of operation, a summative evaluation should be conducted.

Establishing the Program at Township High School District 214

Often, districts experience a shock when they receive a large, rapid influx of new English language learners into their schools, especially if they do not have experience addressing the distinct needs of these students. This may occur if the districts have had few ELLs in the past or if the new group has considerably weaker academic skills than previous groups of ELLs. Such an influx occurred in Township High School District 214, a suburban area west of Chicago in Arlington Heights, Illinois, which was experiencing secondary migration (i.e., immigrant families leaving their urban port of entry, in this case, Chicago). This

Midwestern school district operates six high schools serving approximately 12,000 high school students annually. Of these students, about 800 are English language learners; 120 to 150 each year are new arrivals to the United States. There are 39 language groups represented in the district. Hispanic students make up 70-75% of the English language learners; 3-4% each are Gujarati, Korean, Polish, and Russian. Other groups have smaller percentages.

Dennis Terdy, the district's director of grants and special programs, took the initiative to work with other school administrators to examine the options for helping the newcomer students. As he met with ESL coordinators, division heads, foreign language supervisors, associate principals, and the assistant superintendent for educational services, they made a decision to explore the possibility of establishing a newcomer program.

One step they took was to visit well-established newcomer programs that were similar to their draft design to discover best practices. They realized that even though the programs they visited were quality programs, some aspects needed to be adapted to fit their own specific local conditions. However, many other ideas could be adopted in their program.

Another critical step was to gain the endorsement and commitment of the school board. In Township 214, support for the newcomer program began when Terdy met with the board regularly in the initial planning stages to outline the program design and present the rationale for it. In these sessions, he was also able to orient the board members to the needs of the newcomer students and examine programmatic alternatives. Gathering information and presenting research on newcomer programs was also essential. Terdy utilized information from the Center for Applied Linguistics' research study in particular.

Another very important aspect of establishing the newcomer program was publicizing and disseminating information about it. To accomplish this, Terdy met with every group in the district—board members, administrators, teachers, parents—and gave each group the same information in order to build consensus. He also held three community forums sponsored by the schools.

Once the decision to go forward with the newcomer center was made by the school board and administration, funding sources needed to be tapped. While some local and state support was available, Mr. Terdy also wrote a successful grant proposal to a U.S. Department of Education Title VII program competition.[3] This provided the seed money to develop the program more fully and to cover many operational costs for the first few years.

The administrators and policy makers in Township 214 decided to create a short-term program lasting from one semester to 1 year (depending on student need) at a separate site. In addition to the two semesters of the school year, a summer session would be offered. From 120 to 150 students were expected to be served annually. The site would be centrally located and also act as the district intake center. When students arrived in the district, they would first register formally in their home high school. Students indicating that they had been in the United States for 3 years or less and spoke a language other than English would be referred to the newcomer/intake center for further assessment. These assessments would include open-ended and structured interviews in English, a low-level reading exam, and a writing sample in English. Spanish-speaking students might also be asked to read and produce a writing sample in their native language to assess their native language literacy. The program planned to use the *Spanish Assessment of Basic Education (SABE)* to measure Spanish reading proficiency.

The newcomer program in Township High School District 214 was designed to provide an efficient process for new immigrant students at the secondary level to belong to a group and to make the transition into the regular ESL program more smoothly. This system allows the students to accelerate their learning of English while receiving credit for the

---

[3]This grant competition ceased in 2001 after the No Child Left Behind Act of 2001 was passed and Title VII was reorganized as Title III. The Title VII supervising agency, the Office of Bilingual Education and Minority Languages Affairs, was renamed the Office of English Language Acquisition, Language Enhancement and Academic Achievement for LEP Students.

classes they take, thus preparing them for high school graduation. Two courses, human geography and life skills, carry core content credit, while others, such as introduction to ESL, carry elective credit. If algebra is offered, it also carries core credit. In addition, each teacher is assigned responsibility for one cohort of students, following current research that shows that small, cohesive groups of high school students seem to work best in promoting a sense of belonging. As a result, teacher-student relationships are closer, which has a positive impact on attendance and on grades.

There are three times during the year when students may exit the program: at the end of the first semester, at the end of the regular school year, and after the summer session. In addition, staff may recommend exit for individual students at other times based on reading and writing scores. The students then make the transition into the high schools' ESL programs.

To facilitate this transition, the newcomer center provides a regularly scheduled orientation day for students who are making the transition to their home high school. The home school also provides an orientation at the end of the school year for newcomer students who will enter the following fall. Each of the six high schools has a counselor who serves the English language learners and who is involved in the transition process. Nonetheless, one of the most challenging aspects of Township 214 Newcomer Center is coordinating schedules with the larger, well-established ESL programs in the six home schools, because each of the schools has its own distinct program.

The newcomer staff are bilingual or ESL certified and were hired by the newcomer program director, who also mentors them. Township High School District 214 provides extensive professional development for all staff, including those at the newcomer center. They attend weekly staff meetings at the newcomer center, and bimonthly meetings are provided at the Illinois Resource Center in nearby DesPlaines through a project funded by the state, covering topics such as curriculum, class management, and methodology. Financial support is available for newcomer staff to attend national conferences.

At a 2002 district-level brainstorming session, attended by board members and administrators (including Mr. Terdy), each person was asked to list and comment on two or three accomplishments of the past year. All of the board members who were present included the newcomer center on their list of district accomplishments. This was an important outcome, demonstrating strong support for the program and recognition of its value to the district. Mr. Terdy expects the newcomer center to continue in the district into the foreseeable future.

Summary

Establishing a newcomer program is a complicated but rewarding process. This chapter has explored program features that need to be in place across all program models and offered a checklist of steps to address when designing a newcomer program. It is a fluid process, and planners need to be aware that design features might shift as the planning and implementation phases unfold. However, without a clear vision for the program, the involvement of key stakeholders, committed staff, and an eye on the ultimate educational goal for the newcomer students, a newcomer program will struggle to take root and thrive. The case of Township 214, however, demonstrates how careful planning can yield a well-regarded newcomer program.

At César Chávez Multicultural Academic Center in Illinois, students study science through English and Spanish.

With the assistance of a local artist, students at Liberty High School in New York City designed and painted this mural in the school's entry hall that depicts U.S. history and immigration.

Students at the International Newcomer Academy in Texas display a quilt they made in one of the school's many clubs. The students donated and distributed their quilts to a local community organization.

Case Studies of Three Well-Established Newcomer Programs

The newcomer study has significantly changed the district program by providing insight into similar programs on the national level. We have provided the administrators, principals, and school board with vital information regarding the target group of students.

—Bilingual Newcomer Center, Anchorage (AK) School District

Introduction

As we stated in chapter 1, one goal of this book is to provide information that educators can use to develop and implement a new program or improve an existing one. So far we have presented findings from research conducted on newcomer programs, described design features, and offered guidance on establishing a program. As was seen in chapter 2, there is a great deal of variability in newcomer program designs, depending on the students' backgrounds, the resources available within the school district, and the size of the newcomer population. District staff have many options when creating a program; the checklist and explanations in chapter 3 can help organize their planning. Now, in chapter 4, we will move from planning to operation and showcase three well-established newcomer programs chosen from our case study research. Each of the featured programs represents a different program design; our discussion highlights the commonalities and differences among them. The matrix in Table 4.1 (pages 80-81) illustrates at a

TABLE **4.1**■

	César E. Chávez Multicultural Academic Center
School and grade level	Middle school Grades 5-8
Site model	Program within a school, full day plus afterschool, year round
Length of enrollment	More than 1 school year
Students' native languages	Spanish, Polish
Instructional program design	Bilingual
Languages of instruction	English, Spanish, Polish
Instructional content courses	Content in native languages, cross-cultural/orientation to the United States, sheltered content in English
Assessments	*Key Math, La Prueba de Realización, Woodcock-Muñoz Language Survey, Illinois Measure of Annual Growth in English, Iowa Test of Basic Skills*
Transition options	César E. Chávez Junior Academy (ninth grade), local high school bilingual program, or other high school program
Funding	Federal and private funds

Liberty High School	International Newcomer Academy
High school Grade 9	Middle school and high school Grades 6-12
Separate site, full day	Separate site, full day
1 to 3 semesters	1 school year
Arabic, Cantonese, Haitian Creole, Mandarin, Polish, Spanish, and others (over 20 languages)	Albanian, Serbo-Croatian, Spanish, Vietnamese, and others (8 to 10 languages)
ESL, bilingual, native language literacy	ESL, native language literacy
English, Spanish, Cantonese or Mandarin, Polish	English with native language support, Spanish (native language literacy classes only)
Sheltered content in English, content in native languages, career education, cross-cultural /orientation to the United States	Sheltered content in English, content in native language (Spanish), career education, cross-cultural/orientation to the United States
Language Assessment Battery, New York State Regents Exams	*California Achievement Test, IDEA Proficiency Tests, Student Oral Language Observation Matrix, Texas Reading Proficiency Test in English*
Student's choice of over 220 high schools in New York City (bilingual, ESL, or mainstream programs or GED program)	Area home schools (middle school and high school) with ESL centers
Federal and state funds, New York City tax levy (local funds)	Federal and local district funds

Key Features of Newcomer Project Case Study Sites

glance the main features of these programs. Contact information for all of the programs can be found in Appendix B.

Our first case study program, the Newcomer Center at the César E. Chávez Multicultural Academic Center in Chicago, Illinois, offers full-day and afterschool instruction in a program within a school for Grades 5–8. It operates on a year-round schedule, and students may remain in the program longer than 1 year. The program serves newcomers whose educational achievement upon entry is below grade level; most are Spanish speakers, a few are Polish speakers. Instruction is delivered through a bilingual design, with content classes in Spanish and Polish. ESL classes are part of the design; for students who have remained in the program for several years, some sheltered content classes in English are also provided.

The second program, Liberty High School, is a ninth-grade, full-day program housed at a separate site in New York City. Most students remain in the program for 1 year. Those who lack formal education in their native language remain for an additional semester. The Liberty program is quite large, with flexible offerings according to the students' native languages and academic experiences. For instance, Liberty offers an ESL track with sheltered content instruction in English for some students; a bilingual track for preliterate Spanish-speaking students, with content courses in Spanish and courses in native language literacy; some content classes in Mandarin or Cantonese (depending on student background) and Polish; and a track to prepare students for the workplace. More than 20 languages are represented among the students at Liberty High School.

The final case study, International Newcomer Academy (INA) in Fort Worth, Texas, is a full-day, separate-site program that serves both middle school and high school students primarily for 1 year. Most of the students are Spanish speaking, but 8 to 10 languages are normally represented each year. Except for a basic literacy class, the middle and high school students have separate classes. INA operates an

ESL-designated program with sheltered content instruction courses. However, some Spanish-speaking students have the option to study Spanish language literacy. INA also offers optional afterschool clubs for the students.

All of the programs in this chapter provide a full-day program for newcomers, which means they can offer a wide range of content and ESL classes. Each program has special courses or curriculum units to help orient students to the U.S. school system, their community, and American culture. In 1999-2000, these three programs received federal funding, to which they added funds from private, state, and local sources.

César Chávez Multicultural Academic Center

It hasn't been easy to initiate the program. The staff has worked well together and Erica [the program director] has promoted team building. Parental support and parental programs are strong. Students are making the transition out of newcomers at or above grade level in native language. They are doing well in English, too, as shown on the Illinois Measure of Annual Growth in English (IMAGE). *How we deliver education here is different. Also teachers are empowering themselves.*

—Sandra Traback, Principal

Program History

The newcomer program at the César Chávez Multicultural Academic Center in Chicago is a bilingual middle school program. Established as a program within a school in 1996, it serves primarily Spanish-speaking immigrant and refugee students in Grades 5-8. It is a full-day program that uses a bilingual education approach. The program is supported through federal education funds under Title VII, with a small amount of private support, including foundation grants. Chávez operates on a year-round schedule: Students have classes for 3 months, then have a 1-month vacation before returning to school for another 3 months.

Students also have the option of attending intersession courses during the breaks.

The principal, Sandra Traback, created the newcomer program at Chávez with the help of Erica Cuneen, who became the first program director. Ms. Traback wrote a successful Title VII grant proposal to the U.S. Department of Education to fund a dual language program with Spanish and English instruction. She also hoped to address other concerns, including how to meet the needs of students who enrolled mid-year and were significantly behind other students their age. She entered into discussions with staff of the Chicago Public Schools Department of Languages and Cultures, which was interested in pursuing newcomer programs. They agreed to create a newcomer program at Chávez with dual language methods. Their initial challenges involved recruitment of students; issues related to planning, such as curriculum development and the identification of appropriate materials; and teacher recruitment.

The Chávez staff examined many newcomer programs and visited the Liberty High School program in New York City, but they tailored the Chávez program to fit their student needs. They wanted a bilingual and comprehensive ESL approach, not a typical transitional bilingual education program. They opted for a full-day design to ensure that science and social studies would be taught, along with English and mathematics, to prepare students for standardized tests. Spanish language arts classes were an unequivocal part of the design as well. They targeted students who had been in the United States for no more than 3 years, had experienced interruption in their formal education, and were at risk in adjusting to their new language and school environment.

To develop momentum for the first year of the program, the director and other newcomer staff visited six schools in the vicinity to describe the new program. They also went into the community to recruit students, speaking with parents personally. Most of the students during the first year came from the neighborhood. Over the years, Chávez staff have worked with the Department of Languages and Cultures to recruit students by writing letters to schools and parents. By 1999-2000, Chávez needed to maintain a waiting list.

School Context

The César Chávez Multicultural Academic Center is a regular public school that serves Grades PreK-9. It offers a wide variety of programs:

Grades PreK–3	dual language program (English/Spanish) that follows a two-way immersion model
Grade 4	transition from dual language to English-medium instruction
Grades 5–7	English-medium instruction, with Spanish maintained by a combination of Spanish enrichment (for native Spanish speakers) and Spanish as a foreign language (for native English speakers)
Grades 5–8	the Newcomer Program for recent immigrants to the United States who have limited English proficiency and interrupted prior schooling
Grades 8–9	the Freshman Academy, an English-medium program that affords students a full school year of transition from middle school to high school in which they can mature, bolster their content knowledge, and strengthen their determination to complete high school
Grade 9	the Newcomer Academy for recent immigrants at the ninth-grade level or for those moving up from the Grades 5-8 newcomer program who need more time before making the transition to a regular high school

Chávez has to contend with many of the serious issues found in other large urban school districts. It is located in the Back of the Yards area of Chicago, not far from the stockyards and railroad yards. The neighborhood is very poor, and most families do not have health insurance. African American and Hispanic gangs are active in the neighborhood, and the school is located between two gang areas. However, school attendance is generally good because the school offers a safe haven for the students and tries to provide outreach and support for their families. There is a high mobility rate (approximately 35%); many families move out of the neighborhood for safety reasons and for better jobs.

Chávez also faces overcrowding. As with many programs in inner city settings, finding space for the newcomer program is an ongoing challenge. The school was built to accommodate 550 students, but by 1998, enrollment was at 800. Chávez has approached the problem in two ways: (1) by operating on a year-round calendar with different tracks for its programs and (2) by finding supplemental space. As a result, Chávez's programs are located in two buildings several blocks apart.

The main building was built in early 1993 and has a Mexican-style entrance with pyramids and bright colors. The second building is an older, leased building that had not been well maintained. From 1996 until 1999, the newcomer program (averaging about 60 students per year) was located in this annex and shared the space with the pre-kindergarten program (120 students) and two kindergarten classes (40 students). During these years, the students in the newcomer program had to walk to the main building several times per week for physical education, library, and computer classes. This situation resulted in lost instructional time and concern for the children's safety, although the school never had an incident during the journeys.

In 1999, the Chicago Public Schools bought the annex and repaired it. Programs at Chávez were relocated, and the Grade 5–8 newcomer program for the 1999-2000 school year was placed in the main building with the preK–5 grades. Grades 6–9 and the ninth-grade newcomer academy were housed in the renovated annex. While some staff would have preferred placing the newcomer program with the middle school students and remaining in the annex, the administration saw several advantages to its decision:

- Newcomer students have immediate access to the computer lab, library, and gymnasium and do not need to move between buildings.
- The classrooms are roomier and provide an atmosphere conducive for studying.
- Afterschool programs take place at the main building and include opportunities for mainstream and newcomer students to interact.
- The curriculum for the newcomer program is closer to the elementary curriculum.

The newcomer program staff has had to make concerted efforts to maintain communication with the middle school program in the annex and to plan meaningful integration of the newcomer and mainstream students. The integration of the student groups is hindered not only by the physical separation, but also because the regular middle school program is on a different academic track. Therefore, the students have intersessions at different times and complete the school year in different months.

Student Demographics

In 1999-2000, the full César Chávez Multicultural Academic Center served more than 900 students, 10% of whom were African American. Approximately 68% of the students were classified as limited English proficient (LEP), with most being of Hispanic origin. A small number of Polish-speaking students were enrolled at Chávez, some in the mainstream program, others in the newcomer program. The ninth-grade newcomer program also had a few Lithuanian and Portuguese students that year. Approximately 10% of the LEP students arrive as newcomers each year. About 80% of the student body at Chávez is eligible for free or reduced-cost lunch.

For most of the years that the Chávez 5-8 newcomer program has operated, it has served primarily Spanish-speaking students from Mexico. Although the program was designed for 60 students, it enrolled 66 newcomers in 1999-2000 and maintained a waiting list. Most of the students were Spanish-speaking students from Mexico; a few were from Guatemala and El Salvador; four were from Poland. The students ranged in age from 10 to 14 and had spent no more than 3 years in another U.S. school, had little or no English proficiency, and had large gaps in their formal educational backgrounds. All of the participating students were eligible for the free/reduced-price lunch program.

Many of the students lived with extended families, including grandparents, aunts, uncles, and cousins. In several cases, parents had worked in the United States for several months to several years before bringing their children to Chicago, so the students were going through a double adjustment process: living in a new country and living with parents who had been absent from their lives for an extended period. The educational backgrounds of the parents varied, but some had very limited formal education.

The program has established 10 admission criteria for newcomers. To enter the program, students must meet at least seven of these criteria. Upon enrollment at Chávez, all students are assessed to determine their current level of educational achievement. They represent a range of abilities. Many of the students' placement tests have shown them to be 2 or more years below their age cohorts. They are usually at the third-grade level or lower when they enter the program. In 1999-2000, only two eighth graders tested at grade level in their native language.

> **Ten Admission Criteria**
> - Newly arrived from a non-English-speaking country
> - Limited English proficiency (Category A or B)
> - Eligible for placement in Grades 5-9
> - Born or primarily raised outside of the United States
> - Enrolled 3 years or less in a U.S. institution
> - Limited schooling interrupted by traumatic events
> - Unfamiliar with U.S. culture and school system
> - Native language skills 3 years or more below grade level
> - Signs of low self-esteem
> - Less than age-appropriate education

Schoolwide, Chávez has maintained close to a 94% attendance rate. The students in the newcomer program average a slightly higher rate, closer to 96%. The dropout rate for both the school and the newcomer program has been zero.

Program Design

The Grades 5–8 newcomer center is designed as a 3-year bilingual program for Spanish-speaking students. The administration chose a 3-year time frame to give the students a greater chance to catch up to their age-level peers and to provide the newcomer students with the skills they need to succeed at the high school level and in the world at large. This transitional program offers ESL classes and core content classes in Spanish. The program combines several educational reform strategies— looping,[4] small school, and teaming[5]—and provides opportunities for newcomer students to mix with other Chávez students, which has aided the newcomer students' integration and acculturation.

One goal of the program is to bring students as close to grade level as possible in their educational achievement. Another goal is for students to become bilingual in Spanish and English. To help meet these goals, the program offers the students extended time for learning. With the year-round calendar, students have class for 3 months, then have 1

---

[4]Looping involves a class of students staying with the same teacher for more than 1 year.
[5]Teaming refers to a system in which students and teachers are grouped into instructional teams.

month off. However, all newcomer students are expected to attend the half-day intersession classes that are available during their month of vacation. In this way, almost all of the students attend school for 12 months each year. Moreover, the program has developed afterschool enrichment with some activities designed just for newcomers and others for both newcomer and mainstream students.

The program was also designed to increase the amount of English instruction students receive over the 3 years. Whereas in their first year, students might have only one course in English, by the third year half of their instruction would be provided in English. This was not always realized, however, given variables such as students' educational background, native language proficiency level, age, teacher background, and instructional resources.

Originally, program enrollment was set at 60 students, with three cohorts of approximately 20 students per class. Three teachers provided instruction, each specializing in one subject area. Every year, student groupings depended on student age and enrollment percentages. For example, in 1998-1999, one cohort was established for Grades 5 and 6, another for Grade 7, and a third for Grade 8. For the first few years, students were grouped according to their academic level in their native language into beginner, intermediate, and advanced achievement groups. Each group had a mix of ages and levels of English proficiency. Students received content area instruction in Spanish and English language arts instruction in English.

The program evolved over time as it encountered new student needs and learned of successful practices at other schools. In 1999-2000, the students were grouped in two ways. The first period of the day was set aside for an ESL class known as Walking English. Students were assigned to the beginner, intermediate, or advanced class according to their level of English proficiency. Consequently, there was a mix of grade levels in each ESL class.

After first period, the students were reorganized by grade level and went to their respective classes with the three newcomer teachers. Within each grade level, the mix of English proficiency levels and levels of native language ability posed a challenge to the teachers for creating multilevel lessons that would meet all the students' needs. However, the teachers found that they had fewer discipline problems when the students were divided according to grade level. The students studied mathematics, science, social studies, and language arts in Spanish and had another period of language arts in English. The two periods of ESL enhanced the students' English language acquisition. In addition to the core subjects, students took electives such as computer lab, library, and physical education classes with mainstream teachers of those classes.

The Chávez newcomer program has taken advantage of the program-within-a-school design, enabling students to participate in Title I, special education, and physical education classes; use the library facilities; and work with the school's four resource teachers and the regular school counselor, who is bilingual in Spanish and English. Staff create opportunities for the newcomer students to interact with English-speaking students. For example, newcomer students join English-speaking classmates for grade-level field trips and afterschool activities such as dance, sports, and cheerleading. They have email pen pals with students at their grade level in the Chávez mainstream program. Newcomers have participated in projects with younger students at the school as well, such as the community garden and reading partners. For the latter, newcomer students read stories to students in Grades K or 1 and may choose to read in English or Spanish.

The newcomer students also interact with fluent-English-speaking students during the intersession courses, which were originally developed for mainstream students who needed additional academic support. For all students in the grades that correspond to the state's testing program (native and nonnative English speakers alike), intersession courses are geared to reading and math skill development and test preparation.

The enrollment of Polish-speaking students in the school was a new phenomenon in 1999-2000. Due to the low English proficiency levels of the Polish newcomers, they attended English classes with the Spanish-speaking students part of the day and received instruction in Polish from the Polish-speaking teacher for other courses, such as social studies.

Curriculum and Instruction

The curriculum units for the newcomer courses were designed primarily by the program director and the three teachers who initially taught in the program through a partnership with DePaul University staff. In the early years of the program, the curricula for the beginning Spanish group was tied to the Chicago frameworks for third grade, the curricula for the intermediate Spanish group was tied to the fourth- and fifth-grade frameworks, and the curricula for the advanced Spanish group was tied to the fifth- and sixth-grade frameworks. Students are expected to master a set of skills for each subject, although these skills may vary from year to year depending on the educational background of the students. The skills are drawn from the Chicago frameworks and from national standards, such as those of the National Council of Teachers of Mathematics.

The teachers pointed out that the mismatch between students' background knowledge and the background knowledge needed to succeed in U.S. schools has made it challenging to coordinate newcomer curricula with the Chicago content-area curriculum frameworks and to find appropriate instructional materials. Aware of the need to generate a more established set of curricula and materials for newcomers that would be more closely aligned across the various school programs to help meet these challenges, the Chávez administration appointed a curriculum coordinator in 1999-2000. The coordinator's role has been to collaborate with teachers from the various programs at Chávez to refine the curricula and to provide staff development on these changes.

It was also during the 1999-2000 school year that teachers began to incorporate the Chicago ESL standards into the ESL curriculum. Because the majority of the newcomer students are working below grade level and have limited English proficiency, the teachers believed it was not feasible to cover all of the standards covered in mainstream classes. So they chose the most important themes in the content areas and adapted the fourth-grade curriculum for Grades 5 and 6, the fifth-grade curriculum for Grade 7, and the sixth-grade curriculum for Grade 8. When possible, the teachers have aimed for a thematic approach so that each course reinforces the content students are learning in their other courses. Guiding questions and key vocabulary linked to the thematic units are distributed to students biweekly.

For the intersession courses, there has not been a set curriculum. Intersession courses are delivered in English for all students who need additional academic support. For students in the grades that corresponded to the state testing program prior to the passage of NCLB (state testing requirements have since changed), intersession courses for both native and nonnative English speakers were geared to developing reading and math skills and to test preparation. In these courses, newcomer students in sixth and eighth grade had two periods per day of intensive instruction.

The newcomer program is designed to provide instruction in Spanish for content area classes. However, the Spanish proficiency of the teachers has varied over the years, and in some cases, the students have received more instruction in English than originally anticipated. In keeping with the bilingual philosophy of the program, the teachers use Spanish-language textbooks and other instructional materials such as teacher-made worksheets in Spanish and English. The Polish students (who, because they were so few, had to be grouped with Spanish-speaking students) used English texts in the Spanish medium courses;

the Polish-speaking teacher worked with these students in a small group in the classroom.

Given the mixed backgrounds and proficiency levels of the students, the teachers work diligently to develop the students' background knowledge. An emphasis on vocabulary development and a thematic approach support this objective. The teachers often use cooperative learning techniques in their classes so stronger students may help the less proficient ones. Teachers often provide individualized instruction to lower-level students. In 1999-2000, a bilingual aide was available to work with students who were having difficulty in math, science, and Spanish language arts classes.

Across the courses, teachers utilize technology and incorporate reading and writing activities. They use such techniques as graphic organizers, the writing process, hands-on materials, and role plays to support the students in their language and content learning. In addition, the teacher of the grade-level ESL classes tried to present the same grammar points in English that the Spanish language arts teacher was presenting in Spanish. The ESL teacher also planned instruction to pre-teach or reinforce in English some of the math and science content the students received in Spanish.

In practice, the integration of language objectives in the content courses has been uneven. None of the teachers had been trained in sheltered instruction before beginning work at Chávez, and professional development opportunities have not been specifically targeted in this area. The balance between learning through Spanish and learning through English is not a fixed percentage and varies by teacher and subject. The goal of the program is to increase the use of English in the content courses as the students make progress through the grade levels, so that they are prepared to make the transition to English-medium classrooms.

Student Assessment

The newcomer program at the César Chávez Multicultural Academic Center assesses students for several reasons: (1) to determine eligibility for the newcomer program; (2) to evaluate students' native language, English, and math skills; (3) to determine achievement and promotion from grade to grade; (4) to assess students' readiness to exit the program; and (5) to comply with state testing mandates.

When students enter the newcomer program, they take a diagnostic test in math: *Key Math A* or *Key Math B.* This test is available only in English; however, students are given a simple oral translation in Spanish for the word problems. Their scores help determine their placement in the program. The students take the test again near the end of the year to measure their achievement.

Students entering the program in the beginning years were also given the *Woodcock Language Proficiency Battery* for diagnostic purposes. However, it was discontinued because the complete battery requires 3 hours to administer. In its place, the newcomer staff use the *Woodcock Language Survey* in both Spanish and English, which takes less time to administer and provides scores in specific areas in reading (e.g., verbal analogies, letter-word identification, etc.). They have found this assessment to be valid for their student population. These norm-referenced language exams are also used in a pre- and posttest manner to determine the students' language growth.

Entering newcomer students are also assessed to determine whether they need special education or gifted and talented services. Special education services are offered in the mainstream program at Chávez, but students identified as gifted and talented need to transfer to another school for appropriate services.

In order to be promoted from one grade to the next, newcomer students must master 75% of the skills listed for each of their courses (i.e., math, language arts, ESL). Each course has a different number of skills, and these change according to level. Students must also demonstrate 1 year's growth in English and Spanish reading and writing as measured by the *Woodcock Language Survey* and meet district policy regarding grade point averages and absences. Some of the teachers have expressed a desire to assess students' English language growth more frequently than once a year. They recommend an assessment at the end of each trimester for planning purposes.

The newcomer students take some of the same tests as other English language learners in the school. One of these is *La Prueba,* a test that is sometimes given to Spanish speakers in Illinois but is not mandated by the state. It is used to measure grade-level equivalency and the rate of language growth in Spanish. Another such test is the *IMAGE (Illinois Measure of Annual Growth in English),* a set of rubrics used to assess the reading and writing skills of English language learners.

A third test given to newcomers as well as to other students at Chávez is the *Iowa Test of Basic Skills (ITBS).* Newcomer students take the *ITBS* initially to establish a baseline measure. They are not required by the state to take this test until they have been in the United States for 3 years. If they have been in the newcomer program for 3 years, they are expected to reach the level mandated by the state (e.g., in eighth grade, they must score at the 6.5 level—i.e., sixth grade, fifth month— or above). Some newcomer students take this test for practice before their third year, and some do well on it. After their third year, if they do not reach the level required, they may retake the test. Students may get individual help from teachers after school, or they may attend intersession classes. A few students have moved into the ninth-grade newcomer program at Chávez to prepare to retake the *ITBS.* If they do not pass, they may repeat eighth grade in the mainstream program (i.e., transition out of the newcomer program) or attend an alternative school. Each student must pass the Iowa test before entering mainstream Grade 9.

Newcomer students also complete an attitude survey in Spanish twice a year, in January and June. Students are asked how they feel about their classes, about school in general, about the amount of English and Spanish they are using, and about their educational aspirations. In 1999-2000, the students began to maintain assessment portfolios. One teacher provided students with orientation to the portfolio process involving the inclusion of 20 homework tasks and 2 reports.

Staffing and Professional Development

The César Chávez Multicultural Academic Center School is staffed by approximately 60 teachers and 40 career personnel (e.g., cafeteria workers). In 1997-98 and 1998-99, the Grades 5–8 newcomer program supported five staff members with teacher status. Three were classroom teachers; one was the administrator of the program; and the other filled several roles, including assessment specialist, intake registrar, family liaison, and guidance counselor. The latter position was supported in part with Title I funding. The administrator was supported in part with Title VII grant money. All staff members were bilingual in English and Spanish.

In 1999-2000, the Grades 5-8 newcomer program had one full-time and one part-time administrator. Three teachers worked full time in the program with one bilingual aide. The three teachers serving the Spanish-speaking students were organized by content area, so each teacher taught every student in at least one core class. Barring personnel changes, this arrangement would permit students to have the same three teachers each year in the program. The Polish-speaking teacher, who was not part of the newcomer staff per se, taught the Polish newcomer students for part of the day.

The newcomer program director, not the school principal, selected the teachers for the newcomer program. This is not an uncommon practice in newcomer centers given the importance of having teachers who understand the immigration process, second language acquisition theory, biliteracy development techniques, and so on. In the case of

Chávez, the director recruited teachers from a local university with a strong teacher education program. Some teachers transferred from other Chicago schools.

Three main criteria were set forth in recruiting: The teachers needed to be bilingual in Spanish and English, certified to teach in Illinois, and have an ESL or bilingual endorsement or certificate. Unfortunately, it was difficult to find staff in the Chicago area who met all of the criteria. This was especially true of bilingual math and science teachers, who rarely had an ESL or bilingual credential. Often, bilingual teachers were hired on a provisional basis while they took courses to earn a bilingual or ESL certificate. Another important criterion was that the individuals hired be able to function well as a team, because they would be working very closely together.

Staff turnover has been a persistent challenge for the Chávez program, however. In principle, newcomer students are supposed to have the same three teachers for their 3 years in the program. This design is similar to the type of looping done in many elementary schools, in which the teacher moves up to the next grade with their students. At Chávez, keeping students with the same teachers for 3 years is designed to help them adjust to a new country and school and to provide close monitoring of their progress and needs. In practice, however, students have not had the same group of teachers every year. In each year since the program began, one or more teachers have left. This staff mobility is not unusual for an urban school, but it does put a burden on the administration to continually recruit new teachers, to foster a team-building relationship among new and old staff members and the students, and to maintain the curriculum development process.

As of the 1999-2000 school year, the newcomer program did not have its own professional development plan. The program administrators have provided mentoring of new teachers for a time. Most of the teachers, however, have managed their individual professional growth through ESL and bilingual certificate programs or masters in education programs. Some funds have been available to teachers for conference attendance upon request.

Parent and Community Outreach

César Chávez provides a range of services to families of immigrant and refugee students, including adult ESL classes and classes in native language literacy, GED preparation, and citizenship. Sometimes older siblings of the newcomer students attend adult classes, providing a positive role model for the younger students and enhancing literacy education within their families.

A parents' lounge in the main building is open during the school day to provide resources and materials for parents. A Spanish-language brochure that presents facts about the newcomer program is distributed to parents, who are also invited to an orientation meeting at the beginning of each school year. A monthly newsletter and written announcements in English and Spanish keep parents informed about school events. The bilingual Polish teacher involves Polish-speaking parents whenever possible. Although parents are not classroom volunteers, they do assist with tasks such as copying and assembling materials, serving on the local school council, and escorting students through the neighborhood to ensure their safety.

The school has set up several effective partnerships with community groups to provide such services as health care, housing, violence prevention, and clothing. The school offers onsite immunizations and dental check-ups provided by the department of health. The dentists receive a stipend for their services, but the services are free to Chávez students. For the first several years of the newcomer program, one administrator acted as the parent liaison and was in close contact with all the newcomer families and helped them navigate some of the local social service programs that were available.

Transition Measures

The program-within-a-school design provides flexibility in the transition process. Having multiple opportunities to interact with mainstream students through field trips, afterschool activities, and intersession courses, and having exposure to mainstream teachers through the elective courses, helps students become acculturated to U.S. schools, which in turn helps them make a smooth transition to a mainstream program.

Students who enter the newcomer program in Grade 5 or 6 may remain in the program for 3 years. Students do not exit the program until they are ready and meet the criteria—that is, they have reached level 6.5 (i.e., sixth grade, fifth month) or are no more than 1.5 years below grade level in English, math, and Spanish. Or, if their English and math levels are 6.5 or above, the minimum level for Spanish is 4.5.[6] The criteria correspond to the program's goal of developing a strong base in the students' native language and the belief that first language proficiency aids second language acquisition. If the students exit the newcomer program before the end of their eighth-grade year, they may enter the English-medium program for middle school students at Chávez itself, where Spanish is taught as a foreign language.

Students who may still need intensive language support, in particular those who entered the program in Grade 7 or 8, have the option to move into the ninth-grade newcomer program at Chávez. Graduating eighth-grade students may enroll in transitional bilingual education classes at the neighborhood high school, or they may attend another high school in a mainstream or ESL program.

In 1999, all of the eighth graders, including the newcomer students, met at Chávez with visiting counselors from the eight area high schools. The counselor at Chávez set up these meetings, which lasted for 2 days, with four high schools represented each day. In these meetings, the counselor from each school gave a presentation to the

---

[6]Because the enrollment of Polish-speaking students was new the final year of our case study, a level had not yet been set for proficiency in Polish as an exit criterion.

students in English. Afterward, the newcomer program administrator met with each student individually to discuss the orientation, and students received a book describing each of the high schools. Through conversations about their interests and aspirations, the administrator helped students choose the school they would like to attend. They discussed the requirements of a 4-year high school and realistic goals for moving forward. This information was shared with parents and other teachers. The students completed their applications and sought recommendations from teachers, and the administrator made sure they had all the necessary items in their files. Most students applied to at least two high schools.

Transition

Eighth graders—
- Meet with counselors from area high schools
- Receive a book describing each high school
- Meet individually with newcomer program administrator to discuss orientation/school choice
- Complete application to schools of choice
- Share information with parents and teachers

Administrator—
- Checks students' files for all items necessary for transition

---

After the students leave the newcomer program, no formal monitoring occurs. Informally, the staff check on those who have entered the regular program at Chávez. However, for those who enroll in other schools, staff learn of their progress only through word of mouth or through visits by former students to Chávez. This is one area that the newcomer staff would like to improve. They have begun looking into an accountability system that would allow staff to monitor student progress, including grades and test scores, through Chávez and into high school. The newcomer director was also working to develop stronger relations with the high schools to enhance the newcomer program's ability to place their students in appropriate high school programs.

Student Achievement

La Prueba is a standardized assessment instrument that is used for both newcomers and other Spanish-speaking students in Illinois. Twenty-four César Chávez newcomer students in Grades 5–8 took the reading section of this test in Spring 1997 and again in Spring 1998. Their average reading growth as demonstrated by the test scores was more than 2 years for each grade level (see Table 4.2). The eighth-grade students reached the highest average growth in Spanish reading with 5.5 years of growth in a single year.

TABLE **4.2** ■

Level	Years of growth in reading Spring 1997 to Spring 1998	Students at or above grade level 1998
Grade 5	5.8 years	43%
Grade 6	2.4 years	42%
Grade 7	4.1 years	60%
Grade 8	5.5 years	60%

Students in Grades 5–8, N= 24
Only newcomer students assessed in both 1997 and 1998 were included in this data.

Average Student Growth on *La Prueba—Reading,* 1997-98

On the mathematics section of *La Prueba,* the results for 27 students in Grades 6–8 who took that portion of the test in both 1997 and 1998 revealed an average growth of 3.6 years for the combined grades. Fifty percent of the fifth-grade students who took the test in Spring 1998 scored at or above grade level although they were below grade level upon entry into the program.

The student growth described in the above data emphasizes the benefit of providing students with instruction in their native language as well as in English when they are below grade level upon entering U.S. schools. César Chávez newcomer students were taught mathematics in Spanish and reading in English and Spanish through ESL and Spanish language arts classes. The staff attribute their students' success in part to the bilingual program design and the extended time available for learning. Most newcomer students attend the afterschool program, which enriches their academic study. Furthermore, because Chávez is a year-round school, most of the newcomer students also attend intersession courses, thereby accelerating their academic learning.

Summary
The bilingual newcomer program at Chávez has benefited the students by allowing them to learn academic content through their native language. The program is also designed to help students develop native language literacy skills. The teachers have been very motivated in the classrooms and seek ways to engage students in the learning process. Given Chávez's success in raising student achievement, there is evidence that good teaching and learning have taken place. With a sustained professional development plan, all teachers could share a depth of understanding about topics like second language acquisition, while specific skills and knowledge in targeted areas could be strengthened in ways that would benefit the program as a whole.

The year-round design of the school and its application in the newcomer program provide an excellent advantage for the newcomer students. We have found in our research, as well as in other research conducted on school reform, that extended time for learning is critical to the success of English language learners, especially those who are not on grade level academically (Cummins, 1981; Thomas & Collier, 2002). The opportunity for intersessions and multiple course options for the newcomer students is a model worth sharing with other sites. Moreover, requiring newcomer students to attend intersessions (specifically test-taking classes) as preparation for the statewide benchmarking tests demonstrates a serious commitment to the students and their educational needs.

The option of having students remain in the program for up to 3 years has helped students make progress in a comfortable, familiar environment. It is a less common program design than we have found in our study, where more than half of the programs have students remain in the program for only 1 school year, or 1 year plus a summer program. However, the combination of programmatic features such as looping, small school, and teaming, and the opportunities for newcomer students to mix with other Chávez students have aided the newcomer students' integration and acculturation.

The Chávez newcomer program needs to continue to align the curriculum to the Chicago and Illinois standards and frameworks. Because the program is relatively long term, and students often make the transition into regular school programs rather than to other ESL or bilingual programs, it is very important to provide a standards-based curriculum to the extent possible. While it can be challenging and frustrating to provide grade-level content to newcomers with limited educational backgrounds, it is a goal to work toward for the students who are in their third year of the program. The Chávez program goal is for students to reach a 6.5 grade level, but many will enter Grade 8 or 9 still needing to accelerate their learning to reach their grade level. Therefore, closer articulation is needed with the receiving schools so that students continue to receive academic and language development support.

The César Chávez Multicultural Academic Center has made an impact on its students' educational lives. In November 1998, Chávez, along with five other schools, received the 1998 Schools of Excellence award from Ryder Systems, Inc., and *Hispanic Magazine*. Chávez was also invited to make a presentation about its newcomer program at the Improving America's Schools conference held in Denver, Colorado, in November 1998, as one of six schools in the United States that was successfully implementing comprehensive school reform and had shown significant gains in students' academic achievement.

Liberty High School

For immigrant youngsters, Liberty High School lights the way to a meaningful education and provides a bridge that leads to a bright future. Liberty is known in New York City as the school that will accept any student who meets the age and language requirements.

—Bruce Schnur, Principal

Program History

Established in 1986 as a ninth-grade high school for new arrivals to the United States, Liberty High School (LHS) has served newcomer students for more than a decade as part of the alternative high school superintendency in New York City. Situated in the Chelsea area of Manhattan, this successful 1-year program supports multiple course options for more than 600 immigrant students. As a separate-site location, this full-day program offers transitional bilingual, native language literacy, and ESL curricula to serve the special needs of its diverse student population. The goal of the program is to prepare students for a smooth transition into the New York City high school system.

In 1995, the LHS program received a 5-year, federally funded Title VII grant (Project NEON) to restructure and upgrade all existing programs and operations at Liberty. As of 1999-2000, the restructuring process was complete, and the program offerings at Liberty had been further diversified to meet the varied needs of its newcomers. Since it was established, Liberty has made it possible for thousands of immigrant youth to continue their high school education upon arrival in New York City. Many of the students have gone on to complete their high school studies after their introduction to U.S. schools at Liberty, and some have also gone on to graduate from college as well.

School Context

LHS occupies a small five-story building in the Chelsea area of Manhattan. A colorful, student-designed mural depicting scenes from

U.S. history and immigration is an eye-catching attraction in the school entrance on the ground floor. The cafeteria and space for vocational activities are also on the ground floor. The second floor houses the administrative offices, and most of the 23 classrooms span the top three floors.

Although the building was not originally designed as a school, LHS staff have made as many adaptations as possible to make the building suit their needs. They converted one room into a quasi-gymnasium to provide an area where the students could, at a minimum, perform calisthenics and aerobics exercises for physical education classes. But space issues limit the types of physical education activities that students and staff can participate in at the school.

Another room was transformed into a school library containing a large assortment of literature and reference books in English and in the native languages of many of the students. The library has multiple computer terminals for students and staff, and a computer lab provides many more terminals. With ingenuity, the LHS staff have utilized the building's limited space to the maximum to provide a variety of programs for high-school-age newcomers throughout the year.

Student Demographics

All of the students at Liberty are English language learners with little or no English proficiency. Many students lack literacy skills in their native language as well. In the 1999-2000 school year, LHS had students from 40 countries, with 21 native languages represented among them. The most common languages among the students that year were Spanish, Cantonese, Polish, Arabic, and Haitian Creole. When Liberty High School was established, the majority of the students were from Hispanic backgrounds; however, in recent years, the student population has become more diverse. While the Hispanic population has decreased, the Bengali population has been growing, from two students in 1995-96 to 30 in 1998-99. The Haitian-Creole population also grew substantially from 1996 to 1999.

The academic levels of LHS students vary widely, but one requirement for entrance into the newcomer program is that students have a maximum of 8 years of previous schooling. Over the past decade, an increasing number of students have enrolled who are less academically prepared than previously or are older than the expected age for ninth graders. Although some LHS students have completed 8 years of schooling, their ages range from 14 to 20.

In 1995-96, 11% of the students (50) lacked native language literacy skills, but in 1998-99, the percentage had increased to 25% (150 students). In 1998-99, the over-age population rose even more dramatically; 33% percent of the students were 17, and about 32% were 18 or older. According to the school's principal, Bruce Schnur, about half of the students in 1999-2000 were at grade level while the other half were below. All of the students in the LHS newcomer program were eligible for free or reduced-price lunch.

Prior to federally funded school reform efforts in 1995, the dropout rate at LHS was 15%. A follow-up study in 1996 revealed that it had been reduced to 4%, and subsequent studies showed that it remained at that rate through 1998. However, the principal, Bruce Schnur, has emphasized that the rate is difficult to determine accurately because of the transient nature of the immigrant population. The student attendance rate has held steady at 91%, and 16 students had a perfect attendance record for 1998-99.

Program Design

The LHS newcomer program is a full-day program designed to provide the New York City ninth-grade curriculum to students who are academically prepared for it, and to provide courses that will accelerate the learning of those who are not yet ready for the ninth-grade curriculum. While students develop their English language skills, they may also develop native language skills and receive acculturation to the school, the city, and the United States. Although the separate-site location limits LHS students' interaction with native-English-speaking peers for a time, one goal of the program is to help students develop their social language and academic skills to prepare them to integrate with native-English-speaking students and meet the academic challenges of a mainstream high school.

The program at Liberty High School is multi-faceted, encompassing four instructional programs and four "houses" within these programs. Over the years, Liberty has designed a complex set of courses for students to address their literacy, ESL, and academic content needs. Students who speak Spanish, Chinese, and Polish have bilingual program options, whereas students from other language backgrounds enter the free-standing ESL program. All students receive ESL instruction and are placed in one of the nine proficiency levels according to their language, age, and academic backgrounds. The ESL levels are described below.

> *Literacy Levels A, B, and C* are designed especially for students whose native language does not use the Roman alphabet. Most of the students in these literacy levels are not in a bilingual program. The exception is Chinese students, who do have bilingual options.

> *ESL Levels A and B* are dual language literacy classes for Spanish speakers who have low literacy skills in their native language. Students receive instruction in both English and Spanish.

> *ESL Levels 1, 1B , 2, and 3* are regular ESL classes. The ESL 1B level is for "false" beginners who have taken ESL 1 but are not yet ready to take ESL 2. Some of the students in these levels are in the World of Work or Multicultural House, described in the paragraphs that follow.

Students who have few literacy skills in their native language enter one of three literacy houses: 1) the mini school for Spanish-speaking students, 2) the Chinese pullout literacy program, or 3) the ESL free-standing literacy program. Students who are above ESL 1 in the regular free-standing ESL program enter one of two tracks: Those who are going on to a full high school enter the science track, and those who are not going to continue high school enter the World of Work. All regular ESL 2 students are in the Multicultural House, which combines ESL, art, global studies, math, and home economics. Content subjects are taught through sheltered instruction in English, or they are taught bilingually in Spanish, Polish, or Mandarin (or Cantonese, depending on the language most of the students from China speak in a given school year). The subjects include math, science, social studies, language arts, and health. The average LHS class size is 20 to 25 students.

Students in the World of Work House are mostly in the over-age group, 17-19 years of age. About 30 students in World of Work participate in unpaid internships. The internship class is a one-period class in which the students learn skills that are necessary for work, such as home economics and art or design. Some students work for local agencies such as community boards and council offices. To enroll in World of Work internships, students must be in ESL Level 2 or 3. The students who participate are usually non-Chinese, non-Spanish-speaking students who have a free period in their academic schedules. Older students (age 19 or 20) who have few high school credits join the Business Academy House. In addition to a double period of ESL, they attend a specially designed, double-period business and survival skills class followed by a single-period, hands-on reinforcement class.

In February 1999, LHS began a pre-GED program for students 17 and older to prepare them for entrance into regular GED programs in area high schools. This program evolved from a need to assist students who had entered regular GED programs but were not successful. Students in the noncredit pre-GED program at Liberty take regular ESL for two periods in the morning. The rest of the day they have a block schedule to develop math and science vocabulary, social studies, English, and test-taking skills.

Many students at Liberty receive credits for high school graduation that will carry over when they make the transition to their new school. Higher-level ESL courses count as English credits. Core content courses such as sequential math (levels I, II, and III) and biology yield credits, too. An ESL level 2 student, for example, may receive 10 core credits in 1 year. If a student attends two summer sessions in addition to the school year, it is possible to earn up to 16 credits, including three per summer.

The afterschool program at Liberty meets during the ninth period after the regular school day and offers students a number of activities, including clubs, tutoring, and additional courses. Clubs change by semester, some meeting two times per week for 2 hours each, others once a week. Some clubs offered at LHS include drama, art, video, guitar, Explorer, and choral music. Students may also take afterschool courses and receive one credit each for video, reading, ESL, or literacy, and one half credit for music. Tutoring is available after school for students to receive homework help in math and literacy. Students may participate in afterschool sports such as bowling and volleyball with 1 or 2 days of practice per week.

As in other effective newcomer programs, students and their families are provided other services as well. Liberty has made arrangements for students to receive access to health care services, such as immunizations and eyeglasses, and employs a social worker to help students and their families on a case-by-case basis. Liberty also provides Title I and special education classes.

A new cohort of students arrives at LHS each semester. Historically, the LHS program has been a 1-year program. However, to accommodate underschooled students who lack literacy skills in their native language, the length of stay may be extended to three semesters. In contrast, students with strong educational backgrounds who make rapid progress learning English may exit after one semester. Program flexibility that allows for individualized scheduling makes it possible to enroll students in the most appropriate classes for their needs in order to maximize the effectiveness of their stay at Liberty.

In 1995, LHS began offering an orientation program in December and May for students who arrive after the beginning of the semester (when the cohort slots are full) and have not enrolled in another NYC school. This orientation program has two main goals: 1) to acquaint the students with their community and prepare them for entrance into the LHS program the following semester and 2) to maintain consistent enrollment levels despite the exit of about 250 students to other high schools at the end of each semester. In order for the LHS program to run smoothly, it must maintain a minimum of students throughout the year. (Additional information on the orientation program is provided later in this chapter.)

The LHS program has operated with state and city education funds, federal funds through the Title I and Title VII programs, and some private funds for specific projects. In 1999-2000, the program received funds from the Office of Refugee Resettlement, U.S. Department of Health and Human Services, for parent meetings that would serve Polish refugee students and to write a physical education curriculum for an afterschool course.

Curriculum

The LHS teachers have collaborated to develop curricula and thematic units for the various instructional programs that take into account the New York State standards. According to the Liberty teaching staff, their instructional programs have evolved as they adapt to meet the needs of the students enrolling at the school from year to year. They have developed the Multicultural House curriculum, the ESL curriculum for levels 1 and 2, and literacy curricula, including English levels A-C and native language literacy in Chinese and Spanish. In addition, cooperative teams composed of members of the ESL staff and native language arts staff have created specialized curricular themes, such as the following:

- *American Culture* (for Multicultural House students) includes global studies, native language arts in Spanish, and language arts in English.
- *New York City as a School* is a math/science unit in a literacy curriculum developed by the teachers of native language arts in Chinese.
- *The Fujianese Community in East Broadway* includes language arts and global studies tied to New York state standards. (There are also plans to develop a curriculum for a Spanish neighborhood.)

Curricula compiled with Title VII funds for other subject areas include a math/science technology program aimed at preparation for the Math Regents 2 test and a dual literacy curriculum with ESL and native language arts in Spanish.

Instruction

The wide variety of instructional programs offered at LHS provides opportunities for the teachers to employ many types of teaching strategies and techniques. For literacy courses, LHS teachers employ strategies that begin with oral language in a conversational style, then introduce written language to match the oral language the students have just learned. Writing instruction begins with guided writing, such as manipulating and following a model to put scrambled words from a sentence in order. After the teachers have provided sufficient scaffolding in the writing process, students progress to writing their own sentences, paragraphs, and compositions. At the higher levels of literacy instruction, teachers will sometimes begin with a text rather than with oral language. Students will be asked to read first, then discuss what they have read, then reread the text so that they go beyond dependence on oral language.

Teachers who provide content instruction in English for students who are not in one of the bilingual programs use a variety of sheltered techniques to make their lessons comprehensible. These sheltered instruction teachers employ many different teaching strategies, depending on the level of language proficiency and literacy skills of the students. In a multilevel classroom, peer helpers are often asked to assist the teacher in reaching students at lower levels.

Typically, sheltered instruction teachers place students in cooperative learning groups and provide practical, hands-on activities. For example, students in an English language arts class may work in small groups of four or five to analyze the aspects of a short story they are studying, each group analyzing a different aspect of the story. After the analysis, the small groups share their findings with the whole class. In a cooking class, students may apply mathematical operations. In an orientation class, students practice filling out forms after the activity is modeled for them.

Additional techniques to make content comprehensible include the incorporation of technology in ESL literacy lessons and the use of art in science lessons. In ESL pre-literacy lessons, teachers use visuals and realia (e.g., phone books, letters of the alphabet posted on cards in the front of the room) to teach new vocabulary, to assist students in learning the alphabet, and even to illustrate abstract classroom rules by displaying posters on the wall with a drawing for each concept. Some teachers use a combination of direct instruction and whole language approaches.

LHS teachers also instruct their students in the use of study skills, for example, teaching them how to follow directions in a physical education class and how to schedule their daily activities while learning word processing skills. Teachers model activities for the students to provide a scaffold that will increase their understanding of the content. Students are given career orientation and are encouraged to think about goal setting and how to get from Point A to Point B successfully to accomplish their goals.

Cultural orientation is integrated into instruction. In a Chinese native language literacy class, for example, the teacher may guide a discussion of conflict resolution in a story from Chinese culture and compare it with acceptable ways to resolve conflict in U.S. culture. In the orientation class, students are introduced to U.S. culture as they learn about the New York City communities and their attractions.

The orientation program for students who come midterm consists of one large class with as many as 120 students per session and continues until the end of the semester. Due to limited classroom space, orientation students receive 2 hours of daily ESL instruction in the cafeteria, where they also receive lunch. Retired teachers and a number of paraprofessionals who speak Spanish, Chinese, and Arabic teach the orientation program classes. After lunch, staff members guide the students on field trips around New York City to acquaint them with the community and to allow space in the cafeteria for students enrolled in the regular programs to have their lunch. On these field trips, the students continue to develop their English language skills.

Assessment

Liberty uses multiple measures, including formal standardized assessments, to assess the newcomers. One such instrument is the *Language Assessment Battery (LAB)*, used to assess students' English or Spanish language skills for placement purposes. If possible, they also write a composition in their native language. For math placement purposes, students take teacher-developed math tests that have been translated into the their native languages. The New York Regents tests are used to assess progress and achievement in science and math for students who are advanced enough to take them.

LHS staff have also developed their own assessment instruments to determine students' placement, progress, and achievement in reading, social studies, and health and to assess their readiness to exit from the program. Teachers have developed pre- and posttests for each ESL level and for mathematics. These tests follow the new academic standards established by the New York State Department of Education and the New York City Board of Education. Authentic classroom tests that measure achievement in ESL and in the content areas are also teacher created.

LHS staff also developed a self-assessment for ESL math in1998 and a multicultural awareness test (revised in 1999) that students take upon entering the program to determine their knowledge of cultures other than their own. An instrument to measure self-esteem was adapted from Coopersmith's *Self-Esteem Survey.* This brief survey assesses students' attitudes about family, education, and self.

In 1998-99, a number of Liberty students took the Regents tests for sequential math (I, II, and III) and biology. Of the students who took the exams, 94% passed sequential math I, 89% passed sequential math II, 100% passed sequential math III, and 51% passed biology. In 1999-2000, 56% of the students who took the biology Regents exam passed. Also, 15 students took math Regents tests, and all of them passed. Most of the LHS students who have taken and passed the Regents test are Asian students who entered LHS at grade level or above.

The principal believes that accountability should be measured differently at LHS than at other schools because it is a short-term alternative high school. He believes the first year or two are the hardest for newcomer students and that in later years they may advance more rapidly. Consequently, their progress during their short stay at LHS is not as evident as the progress of students who are enrolled in a program for a longer period of time.

Staffing and Professional Development

In 1999-2000, two full-time administrators—a principal and an assistant principal—and one part-time assistant principal led the program at Liberty High School. Thirty-nine full-time teachers worked in the program, all certified in ESL or a content area or both. Twenty-two teachers had bilingual certification, and most held a master's degree. One had a Ph.D. The teachers were assisted by 17 bilingual aides from five different language backgrounds and by one monolingual English-speaking aide. Overall, the 1999-2000 staff spoke 41 different languages.

During that year, the program also had two state-certified guidance counselors, as well as two staff members designated as advisors, who provided supplemental guidance and advice, particularly for the students from China. The counselors and advisors at LHS are bilingual in English and Spanish, Mandarin, or Cantonese. In addition, the program has three resource teachers. Liberty hires part-time teachers, some of whom are retired, to lead the orientation program.

To monitor instruction, the principal visits the classrooms informally. The LHS staff attend regularly scheduled department meetings and faculty meetings once per month. Teachers and paraprofessionals may also participate in various types of professional development related to ESL and newcomers, but attendance is not required. Professional development sessions offered at LHS are usually attended by 10 to 20 teachers. If more than 20 plan to attend, the same topic may be offered in two separate sessions. Outside speakers are sometimes invited; at other times Liberty teachers give presentations to their colleagues. Past topics have included teacher sensitivity, state standards, literacy for Spanish and Chinese students, bilingualism, classroom management, working with parents, and technology.

New teachers are required to participate in professional development regarding newcomer students. Teachers who do not have ESL certification are encouraged to participate in professional development for ESL, but they cannot be required to do so. Title VII funds have subsidized staff development, covering tuition for two or three teachers per semester to take university courses in ESL or bilingual education. A number of teachers have taken advantage of this opportunity. In addition, some LHS teachers are learning a second language (Mandarin, Polish, or Spanish). District funds support LHS staff attendance at workshops and conferences.

Parent and Community Connections

Many parents participate in activities and services offered at Liberty. Title VII funding provided workshops for parents throughout the 1999-2000 school year. Bilingual teachers assisted in conducting these workshops, where a variety of topics were covered, including immigration, legal issues, and AIDS prevention.

The development of a parent handbook, *Parents as Partners in Education,* was a project completed with Title VII funds. The handbook was translated into Chinese, Polish, and Spanish and was distributed to the parents of LHS students. Parents are usually invited to PTA meetings two times per semester. Invitations are extended via telephone or in letters that have been translated into the parents' native language. Fifty or more parents at a time have attended these meetings. Topics covered at PTA meetings include learning standards, educational programs, food and health services, summer school programs, and student transfer.

One service offered to parents at LHS is a computer literacy class that they may attend on Saturdays when they accompany their children to the school for tutoring. In 1999-2000, the guardian of one LHS student offered computer classes in a Wall Street office, where 15 students met regularly on Saturdays for 8 weeks. Also, ESL classes for parents meet twice a week in the evening for two levels, beginners and advanced beginners, with approximately 8 to 12 parents in each class.

The community is very supportive of the program at LHS and believes that Liberty is a good neighbor, helping students to succeed. Community members preferred Liberty to a private school when they were presented with school options many years ago. One LHS teacher in particular is very involved with the community, and Liberty frequently participates in neighborhood special events such as the 21st Annual Citywide Chinese Parents' Conference. Community service projects and student internships bring the LHS students into the local neighborhoods.

Transition Measures

The LHS program, as mentioned earlier, begins with a new cohort of students every semester, and some students exit the program at the end of each semester, in January and in June. However, most students stay for two semesters, and many take summer courses as well. Some students with low literacy skills or over-age status remain for three semesters. Upon exit, the students choose a high school from among the more than 220 high schools in New York City. It is a district policy that high school students may attend the school of their choice if they are accepted. If not, they attend the school in their attendance zone.

The LHS guidance counselors and advisors meet with each student to offer individualized education and career planning, helping the students make choices and apply to the high school(s) of their choice. Many of the high schools offer ESL and bilingual education options. A small number of students who have completed the pre-GED courses leave Liberty to attend a GED program elsewhere in the city. Other students return to their country of origin, or they leave New York City and relocate to other U.S. communities. Many over-age students do not finish school but enter the workforce.

Due to the many options students have upon exiting, one of the most challenging aspects of the program has been tracking students after they leave LHS. Although guidance counselors may know which schools students planned to attend, New York City has not had a centralized system to collect data on all students, so counselors cannot track the progress of students once they have enrolled in other schools. Some students do well academically and go on to college, but LHS staff learn about their progress only informally.

Summary

Liberty High School is well known in New York City and in New York State for the accomplishments of both faculty and students. In 1996, eight students and the principal were invited to participate in UNICEF's 50th anniversary celebration at the United Nations. In 1998, a commendable school project was undertaken when Liberty High School received a $50,000 grant and contracted with an area artist to help the students design a tile mural for the entrance to the school building. In 1999-2000, LHS teachers were writing a book about Liberty in which they profiled the various programs within the larger newcomer program.

Another example of Liberty's success is the awarding of a state archives grant. The project had two components: The first was to research the East Broadway Fujianese community and write a curriculum for language arts and global studies tied to NYC standards. Two teachers were involved in this component and developed a Web site for the materials. The second was to hold city-wide workshops that would show teachers how to use the curriculum.

The principal, Mr. Schnur, participates in many conferences throughout the city, including the Over-Age Conference and the Bengali City Conference. Mr. Schnur moderated a panel of LHS students in a symposium at the Bengali Conference. It was one of the most popular sessions of the conference, which motivated LHS to want to return for the next conference and involve as many students as possible.

The greatest accomplishment of Liberty is the educational opportunity it is providing for newcomer students, including those who come to the United States with interrupted formal schooling. According to the principal, the aspects of the program that are working especially well are the literacy programs and the pre-GED program. These programs are addressing the needs of many students who may not be eligible initially for programs in other NYC high schools, but who seek to further their education. As a result of their experience at Liberty, they may go on to succeed in other academic programs or in the workforce.

International Newcomer Academy

The INA community service projects and collaborative academic projects are effective features of this program that make it unique. These projects have enhanced the students' language acquisition in real world situations.
    —INA Staff

Program History

International Newcomer Academy (INA) in Fort Worth, Texas, was established in the fall of 1993 as a pilot program to provide a multicultural learning environment for newly arrived English language learners at the middle school and high school levels (Grades 6-12). As a result of an increase in the newcomer population, the regular school programs had become frustrated in their efforts to satisfy the needs of both the newcomers and the more advanced ESL students. Furthermore, the steady arrival of new students throughout the school year interrupted the flow of instruction. Administrators and teachers came to the conclusion that a specific newcomer program had the potential to address both issues, and plans were made to establish INA. When it began operation, the INA program served about one third of the schools in the Fort Worth Independent School District (FWISD).

Although INA was designed as a stand-alone facility, it was organized to reflect the overall goals of the language centers operated by 16 of the district schools, enabling INA newcomers to make a smooth transition to the language centers upon exiting from the INA program. The stand-alone, separate-site design was chosen for the following advantages:

- A clear, single focus on new immigrant students and their needs
- An environment that offers special support for newly arrived students and encourages risk-taking learning
- Access to district programs, resources, technology, and services that the students otherwise might not have
- An operational structure that allows for site-based decision making regarding scheduling, staff, and curriculum

Initially, the school district had some reservations about the separate-site design because of the potential for isolating newcomer students. However, as the INA program has developed and evolved since 1993, the district has found that the advantages of the separate-site location outweigh concerns about temporary isolation. INA has received strong cooperation from other schools in the district to implement collaborative academic projects to foster interaction between INA students and native-English-speaking students.

At INA, administrators, teachers, and support staff focus entirely on the issues of newly arrived immigrant students. This perspective is not possible in the regular school programs, where immigrant students are one of many populations to consider when decisions are made. Because new immigrants are the only population served by INA, every decision that is made—scheduling, communications, course content, staff assignment, school calendar, parent meetings—is based upon the needs of students and families new to the United States.

INA operates a full-day schedule and is primarily a 1-year program that offers sheltered content instruction in English with native language support, native language literacy instruction in Spanish and Vietnamese, career education, and cross-cultural orientation to the United States. One ESL/social studies teacher, who had a great deal of experience teaching in mainstream schools before coming to INA, commented that the newcomer students feel more comfortable in the INA setting when they find that they are all immigrants with similar experiences. She feels they have a less extended "silent period" at INA than when they are immediately thrust into the mainstream environment.

The INA program initially received federal and district funding, but after it became well established, it began to function entirely through the support of state and local funds. INA's school board has made funding for the program a high priority for state and local sources in order to ensure its continued success.

School Context

When the INA program was established in 1993, it was situated in a working-class, residential neighborhood on the west side of Fort Worth. The immigrant students who came from the more urban areas of the city were transported to and from the INA campus by bus each day. Initially, the INA program was housed in two mobile units on the campus while the adjacent two-story building (a former elementary school) was being renovated. When renovations were completed, the entire program moved into the building.

Over the years, as INA's enrollment increased steadily, mobile units were again added to provide additional classroom and office space. Although INA had outgrown its facilities, the program remained in the old elementary school until 2000-2001, at which time it relocated to its present site, which can accommodate more than 600 students.

The new site offers several advantages. Its central location is accessible to more families, and the program can serve all 16 home schools in the district that have English language centers. Also, INA is now housed with a middle school, the Applied Learning Academy (ALA), although it retains its own administration and a separate-site design. ALA matches INA in its educational philosophy. Staff in these schools planned projects together before INA's move, and with its new strategic location beside ALA, they continue to plan numerous projects that promote meaningful interaction between the newcomers and fluent-English-speaking students in the Academy.

Student Demographics

Fort Worth is a primary refugee resettlement site. Consequently, the newcomers attending INA are recent refugees or other newly arrived immigrant students in Grades 6-12 who have been assessed by the district as beginning English learners. Since INA was established, the majority of the students have been Spanish speakers, but the demographics of other language groups have fluctuated from year to year, depending on the backgrounds of the major immigrant groups entering the United States in a given year. For example, the second largest population attending INA in 1996-97 was Vietnamese, whereas the second largest group in 1999-2000 was Serbo-Croatian.

In 1999-2000, the number of home countries and native languages represented among INA students was between 8 and 10. Approximately 66% of the students were Hispanic, and the most common languages spoken were Spanish, Serbo-Croatian, Vietnamese, and Albanian. The most dramatic change that has taken place in the INA program since it began is the increase in the number of students served, from 50 students in 1993 to 230 in 1996-97 to more than 400 in 1999-2000.

Most students attending INA have received formal education in their native countries, although the population includes some middle- and high-school-age students who have had interrupted schooling. Students may remain in the INA program for up to 2 years if they are preliterate. The majority of preliterate high-school-age students in Fort Worth, however, attend another district program, the Newcomer Career Academy, a 4-year high school that serves approximately 120 students.

Most of the INA students (95-98%) receive free or reduced-price lunches. When many of the students arrive in the United States they are destitute, living with relatives and borrowing clothes and other items they need for survival. The INA guidance counselor facilitates contact between these families and a homeless program in the city that provides the students with some of the personal items they need. The INA staff members are like family to many of the students, and the students rely on them for guidance and support as they make the transition into U.S. culture.

Program Design

The mission of INA is to provide a multicultural learning environment for English language learners that will create a supportive and challenging academic setting where students have opportunities to develop as learners, as effective problem solvers, and as willing speakers of English. The goal of the program is to provide students with a foundation of real-world experiences that will allow them to pursue their lives and educational goals successfully and become contributing, productive members of society.

When the Fort Worth Independent School District established the INA program in 1993, the planners agreed that it would have four distinguishing features:

- Intensive ESL with bilingual support when possible
- Highly trained staff
- A first-year academic foundation to give students the English skills and orientation to U.S. culture and schools needed for progression through the ESL program to the mainstream program
- Entry and exit procedures closely monitored by the district to ensure that INA maintained its role as a transition program, exiting most students to home language center schools within 1 semester to 1 year

For 2 years, before the 1998-99 school year, INA operated on a year-round schedule with intersession course options. The intersessions were offered for 6 weeks (1 week in early spring, 2 weeks in April, and 3 weeks in September), with an additional 3 weeks of summer enrichment. Intersessions were optional; about half of the staff operated the program during these sessions. However, due to district resource allocations, INA returned to a traditional academic-year schedule in 1998-99.

Most students remain in the INA program for a full school year, then enroll in the district's 8-week summer program that offers native language content and sheltered instruction. INA student participation in the district summer program was about 80% in 1998-99. A few students exit the program after one semester if they meet the requirements. Usually, students make the transition to their home school's language center when they leave INA.

High school students in Texas are required to earn a minimum of 21 credits for graduation, and the INA program is designed to help students earn some of their core and elective credits. During one school year, INA high school students may earn a total of six credits: two for math, one for speech, two for language arts (ESL and reading), and one for world geography. This is one or two credits fewer than students in regular high schools typically earn. INA students may earn an additional credit in the 8-week summer enrichment program funded by the district and offered at a language center. The summer program offers classes in biology, algebra, geometry, government, and economics.

In addition to the regular academic program, INA provides other services for students and their families, such as special education classes, tutoring, physical and mental health referrals, parent outreach, community outreach, and partnerships with community organizations. The guidance counselor informs parents and students of their rights to the services offered by organizations outside of INA and shows them how to receive these services. When necessary, the counselor takes students to the service providers and walks them through the procedures for obtaining services. Personal attention such as this illustrates the commitment of the INA staff to the success of their newcomers.

Curriculum
The INA program brochure describes the curriculum as an integrated, thematic approach to language and content learning. It is built upon the concept that students learn best through experience and experimentation. In addition, the INA curriculum values and integrates the cultures, languages, and life experiences of the INA students while providing orientation to the United States and meeting the needs of students who have varying levels of academic preparation.

The curriculum for ESL, reading, and ESL lab courses is based on state essential elements for ESL and reading improvement. It is a sequential language/concept development program reflecting the district's integrated language philosophy. It includes multiple resources, sample integrated units, thematic arrangement, examples of various assessment strategies, and an instructional strategies section that includes explanations and samples of the most effective interactive delivery techniques. Instructional activities develop the students' social and academic skills, with a focus on problem solving and the production of real language and real products.

Instruction

Due to the diversity of native languages spoken by the students, instruction at INA is delivered mainly through sheltered strategies in English. The language/literacy classes include three levels of ESL—preliteracy, middle school, and high school—in the four skill areas: reading, writing, listening, and speaking. Class size is limited to 20 students. Upon arrival at INA, students are placed in a strand—a section of 20 middle school or high school students—and usually remain in that strand throughout their stay. Each teacher is assigned to one strand of students. As new students enroll throughout the year, more strands are formed and additional teachers are hired.

The issue of multiple levels of language proficiency within an ESL classroom is one that teachers find challenging. In particular, this may occur when new students enter the program after the school year has begun. To address this issue, the INA teachers ask student volunteers to serve as peer helpers for the newly arrived classmates. Together, teachers and peers assist the new students to raise their level of English proficiency as quickly as possible. The assistance offered by the peer tutors helps to strengthen and reinforce what the new students have already learned and promotes an attitude of cooperation among the students as they work together to reach their goals.

Scheduling at INA is divided into blue and white days with alternating 90-minute block periods for three periods per day. However, within this system, teachers have the flexibility to extend blue activities into white days and visa versa as needed or as instructionally appropriate. Periods 1 and 2 begin with an advisory-like homeroom. The advisory lasts for 30 minutes of this block at the beginning of the year but is reduced to approximately 10 minutes by the end of the year. Periods 3 and 4 comprise the next block, and Periods 5 and 6 comprise the last block of the day. On Fridays, clubs meet for 1 hour at the end of the day, so the other periods are shortened.

TABLE **4.3** ■

International Newcomer Academy Courses	
Middle School	**High School**
90-minute block, alternating math and science/social studies (white/blue days)	Algebra
	World geography
90-minute block, alternating ESL and reading (white/blue days)	Speech/ESL (*Crossroads Café* video series)
	Reading (ELLIS software)
Art	ESL LAB/keyboarding
Career investigation (service projects)	Career investigation (Vital Link)
Cultural orientation to the United States	Cultural orientation to the United States
School study skills	School study skills

International Newcomer Academy Courses for Middle School and High School

English is the primary language of instruction for all INA students, but preliterate Spanish- and Vietnamese-speaking students take math and language arts in their native language. Native language literacy classes are designed mainly for the middle-school level, although a few high school students may also attend these classes, depending on their needs. Spanish speakers who are literate in Spanish may take a native language literacy class for enrichment during elective time. The middle school classes at INA are all bridge classes, which are tailored to the sixth-grade curriculum and designed to accelerate learning; the standards that are used in curriculum development are the *Texas Essential Knowledge Standards (TEKS)*. The courses for both middle and high school students are shown in Table 4.3 (page 127).

INA teachers employ a variety of literacy development strategies and sheltered instruction techniques. One of the language arts teachers uses videos that have subtitles, such as *Romeo and Juliet,* to develop the students' listening and reading skills as well as their knowledge of literature. Teachers also use techniques such as the natural language approach, cooperative learning groups, Language Experience Approach, Total Physical Response, whole language, student publishing, graphic organizers, visuals, questioning strategies, and aspects of directed instruction to enhance language learning while teaching content. The example below illustrates how some of these techniques are used.

In a multilevel middle-school classroom, the ESL/reading teacher was working with a group of 17 students assisted by a Spanish-speaking instructional aide. Four groups of students with lower-level language proficiency were looking through magazines and cutting out pictures to illustrate free time, schoolwork, and housework. Another group of three students, with higher-level language proficiency, was working on a comparison/contrast paragraph. This group generated ideas comparing free time, schoolwork, and housework in the United States and their home country. First they made a list, then filled in a Venn diagram. After that they composed a paragraph. The teacher gave them a worksheet with key words for comparing and contrasting.

When possible, the staff practice team teaching. For example, two INA teachers, both experienced and certified in social studies and science, alternate days for teaching these subjects. One day Teacher A teaches social studies to one group and science to another group while Teacher B teaches science to the first group and social studies to the second group. The following day they switch groups, allowing both teachers to see all of the students every day and still maintain block scheduling for greater effectiveness.

As mentioned above, school clubs meet for 1 hour on Friday afternoons. A total of 18 clubs offer the students a wide range of activities from which to choose. One example is the cooking club. The students learn how to set the table, make salads and desserts, and serve food. On certain days, INA teachers and students may buy the meals that the cooking club has prepared. Students often learn more about their native cultures in these clubs. For example, in 1999, students in the Asian club learned how to perform Vietnamese traditional dances using decorative fans. Clubs that focus on performance, like dance, drama, and choir, offer performances for INA students and their families and also for students in other schools.

Collaborative Academic Projects

The staff at INA believe it is important for INA students to interact with native English speakers and to have experiences similar to those of mainstream students. To ensure that INA students have these opportunities, one full-time staff member plans academic projects with other schools. Each INA class works with a class of native English speakers to complete a project.

The numerous collaborative academic projects in which the students participate are a unique strength of the INA program. One example was a solar oven project that brought together INA students and students from the Applied Learning Academy in Fort Worth. Another project provided students in beginning literacy classes with opportunities to read to elementary school children or to participate in a pen pal project. One group designed brochures for a business. The example below is an illustration of how a collaborative project works.

In six face-to-face meetings over a 6-week period, INA students and native-English-speaking-students created a multimedia presentation of attractions in Fort Worth entitled, "Welcome to My City." First, the students were introduced to the project and shown how to use PowerPoint software. Next, the sites that would be photographed were randomly assigned to student pairs, who were responsible for preparing the PowerPoint slides of those sites for the final product relevant to their sites. After extensive preparation that included researching the assigned site, informing the other students about it, and taking pictures, students took field trips to the sites. During a subsequent field trip to the Fort Worth Public Library, the students completed the research on the history of their sites. Finally, the students organized the slides into a PowerPoint presentation, adding more information about the sites that would be of interest to newly arriving students and their families. Last, the students created buttons and audio translations of the text in various native languages. Each pair of students was evaluated for their part in the presentation, according to the rubric presented to them prior to the project by the collaborating teachers.

In addition to academic projects, INA students have other opportunities to interact with mainstream students. When the Fort Worth school district held a PTA-sponsored weekend leadership conference for students, five INA students participated along with the vice principal, a counselor, and an instructional assistant. Also, INA students serve in the community twice annually, assisting in various activities that include a food bank, graffiti abatement, senior centers, and park cleanup. The students take community-based field trips and may enroll in the outdoor learning center challenge course, which teaches valuable skills in leadership, teamwork, problem solving, and self-reliance.

Vital Link, a Fort Worth organization, allows students to shadow employees in local businesses for a week to gain insight into real work experiences. INA has adapted its schedule to ensure that students have a Vital Link experience at workplaces such as hospitals, food stores, computer centers, and banks. Career Day is held annually and brings members of the professional community to INA to talk with students. INA staff promote student interaction off campus whenever possible to enhance the students' overall experience and promote integration with other community members of all ages.

Assessment

Multiple measures are used in the INA program to determine the placement, progress, achievement, and exit of students. Placement is determined by scores on several exams: the math component of the *California Achievement Test (CAT 5);* the *IDEA Language Proficiency Test (IPT)* in English or Spanish, which assesses all language skill areas; and district-designed and translated tests. Placement decisions also take into account students' educational background. For Spanish-speaking students, a native-language writing prompt is used. Structured interviews are conducted with students and with their parents at the time of placement to determine attitudes and expectations.

Other assessment instruments used for progress and achievement purposes include checklists, observation tools, portfolios (English writing samples in all subject areas and their rubrics), anecdotal records, rubrics, and more traditional classroom tests. Formal assessment measures include the *Student Oral Language Observation Matrix (SOLOM)* to assess English speaking skills and the *Language Assessment Survey (LAS)* to assess English reading and writing ability. Some students take the state's end-of-course algebra test, but newly arrived students may be exempt from end-of-course tests in Texas for 1 year.

INA departments developed the *Campus Education Improvement Plan (CEIP)* curriculum, which is tied to the *Texas Assessment of Academic Skills (TAAS)* and includes national ESL standards. Students take the TAAS in Grades 8 and 10. The Grade 10 assessment determines whether the students pass or repeat 10th grade. In 1998-99, INA staff designed and implemented standards and assessments in both reading and speaking, although Texas has no state-level ESL standards.

Because most students remain at INA for 1 year or less, exit from the program is based primarily on the amount of time they have been enrolled. Students who have been at INA for one semester to 1 year have their progress reviewed by the entire INA staff. The students' individual portfolios and folders are used in this review process. Students exit at the end of one semester when their portfolios show the following criteria:

- Grades in content-area subjects averaging at least 85%
- Consistent behaviors in English oral language development indicating rapid progress (score 12 or above on SOLOM)
- A minimum of five writing samples assessed at 5 or higher on the district's *Overall Writing Rubric* and work samples demonstrating some understanding of the writing process
- Intermediate level of reading proficiency on the state's reading proficiency tests in English

Students in beginning literacy classes exit from the program after 2 years. Although staff expect that students who exit after 1 or 2 years will have acquired most of the same proficiencies as those who exit at the end of one semester, students are not required to have achieved that level in order to exit from INA. Students are assessed by INA staff at the end of 1 or 2 years and exit to their home school language centers regardless of their skill level. Records are sent to the language center showing the students' progress and current language proficiency and content knowledge. The INA staff, in collaboration with the staff in the receiving schools, plan extensive orientation for INA students when they make the transition to a language center program in a mainstream school.

Staffing and Professional Development

In 1999-2000, the INA program employed 18 teachers, all with content-area certification and 16 with ESL endorsements. The program also employed five long-term substitute ESL teachers with certification, who taught all courses, including ESL, in self-contained classrooms. Five bilingual aides assisted in teaching the Spanish and Vietnamese students. Two program guidance counselors, bilingual in Spanish and English, worked directly with students on health needs, substance abuse, decision making, and more. One full-time administrator and two part-time administrators directed the program.

In general, new staff members are selected through an interview process involving the director and current staff. No staff member is automatically placed at INA by the district central administration. When new teachers are being recruited, three or four INA teachers lead the interview process. Some teachers transfer to INA from district language centers. For others, teaching at INA is a second career. New teachers are assigned a mentor the day they begin teaching at INA, in accordance with district policy for new teachers. In an interview, new teachers at INA expressed their thoughts about mentoring, stating that the most effective mentoring took place when they had opportunities to visit the classrooms of experienced teachers and observe the techniques and management styles they used. INA staff have a low attrition rate, and no teacher has left due to dissatisfaction with the program.

Four focus teams of teachers are designated to address school issues. Each staff member belongs to one of these teams, which provide guidance and direction and form the nucleus of the INA site-based management team. The teams serve as resources for development and implementation of INA concepts and objectives. Table 4.4 below describes the team functions.

TABLE **4.4**

INA Staff Teams	Team Functions
Instruction	Takes responsibility for instructional activities associated with INA's extracurricular/co-curricular plan, including appropriateness of activities and pre- and post-instructional activities.
Parents and Community	Organizes parent meetings and other events, performance programs, Culture Week and Culture Fair, and takes responsibility for Vital Link connections and community service.
Communication	Ensures that all interested parties receive appropriate correspondence about school activities/events in both English and native languages.
Operations and Governance	Provides input for student scheduling, transportation, and budget.

International Newcomer Academy Focus Teams and Their Functions

A great deal of flexibility exists within these focus teams. Individual teachers are free at any time to discuss their problems with the appropriate team, and they work together on a solution. If an issue affects everyone or if input is needed from all the teachers, the appropriate team works with the whole faculty. In such cases, they may take up the issue at a regular faculty meeting.

Teachers participate in extensive staff development along with administrators, counselors, and instructional assistants. Staff meetings are held once a week, with teachers rotating as leaders. Once a week, staff also conduct focus team meetings to work on curriculum development and curriculum mapping. They map the curriculum across subjects and grades among the teachers in the school so they can see where they fit into the full plan. District funds are used for a half day of professional development once a month. Staff development is provided by INA staff, district personnel, and outside consultants. In addition, staff members attend and present at local, regional, and national conferences.

A variety of topics are covered in professional development sessions. Second language acquisition, cultural diversity training, content area training (i.e., math, social studies, science), dimensions of learning, use of technology in instruction, classroom management, and assessment are some of the main topics. Strategies for teaching English language learners are also presented, including topics such as cooperative learning, emergent literacy, thematic instruction, process writing, and content reading and writing.

Parent and Community Connections

Unemployment has been very low in the Fort Worth area, and most parents have taken advantage of the employment opportunities, many holding two jobs. This has made it difficult for them to be involved in INA activities to a high degree, although they are very interested in their children's academic success. Parental participation has been strongest when parents have been invited to attend special events at the school. INA provided transportation for parents to attend special events at the original site because the school was not located on a bus route, and many of the parents had no transportation of their own. INA staff have considered ways to improve parental involvement. One plan was to offer more educational classes for the newcomer parents in their neighborhoods, thus making the classes more accessible, especially to those without their own transportation.

As mentioned previously, INA students serve in the community twice annually, assisting in a variety activities. INA staff promote student inter-action off campus whenever possible to enhance the students' educational experience and promote integration with other community members of all ages.

Transition Measures

Throughout the school year, INA students engage in activities that strengthen their bond with their home schools. One activity is to visit the home schools and receive orientation to their programs. Eighth graders attend high school orientation sessions especially for them, where they have opportunities to speak with former INA students. Also, the INA guidance counselor meets with transferring students individually to plan their transition to the home school.

Several INA students who were preparing to make the transition to their home schools in May 1999 expressed their thoughts about their INA experience and upcoming transition in an interview with CAL researchers. Mirsada, a ninth-grade student from Bosnia, said that at first it was difficult to make friends, but being at INA was very helpful for her to learn how to adjust to school in the United States. She added that the counselors had spoken to them about making good friends and about the daily routine in the home schools they would attend after leaving INA. Berenice, a 10th-grade student from Mexico, said she liked INA very much. She had lots of friends at INA and felt good there, but she understood that it was time to transfer to the high school so she could improve her English more, and she felt that she was ready. Berenice said the counselor encourages the students when they make the transition to the home school and helps them deal with their concerns.

When INA students are ready to exit the program, the INA vice principal and representatives from the middle schools and high schools in their attendance areas assist the students in filling out course selection forms for the coming year. After students leave INA, they are monitored through the district's research and evaluation department, and data are collected on their progress.

Program Evaluation

The ESL department of the Fort Worth Independent School District has conducted studies to compare INA student data with data from new immigrant students living in areas of the city that were not previously served by the INA program. Previously, newcomer students enrolled directly in an ESL language center. One study demonstrated that INA students remained in the home schools for a longer period of time after leaving INA than did students who entered the language centers directly, indicating fewer dropouts for the INA group. The 1997-98 data revealed that former INA students passed a higher percentage of middle school and high school courses in English, math, and science than did the comparison group. Also, a higher number of former INA students enrolled in high school honors courses.

Summary

INA staff pointed out several aspects of the INA program that they believe are working very well. One is the attendance rate, which remains around 94%. Due to extended class time, high school math students have experienced greater achievement than they had previously. For the state-mandated, end-of-course algebra test, INA had one of the highest scores in the district. Also, the community service opportunities have enhanced the students' language acquisition.

The INA school program and the students have received recognition from the community for their achievements. For example, middle school students have received art awards. The program also received an Excellence in Language Center Award of $10,000, a district award sponsored by Pier One. INA staff and school district administrators have found that the INA program has produced the desired results in improving education for the district's newcomers. INA is meeting its goals and fulfilling its mission as an alternative secondary school that prepares newcomer students to integrate into the larger Fort Worth school system.

INA has demonstrated success in providing a quality program for Fort Worth's newcomer students. One indicator of success has been strong district support, including financial support, and collaboration with other district schools (elementary, middle, and high schools) in providing instruction that integrates INA students with mainstream students on a continuing basis. The low staff turnover is another indicator of success. In an interview with CAL researchers, INA staff indicated that they found it professionally satisfying to have an active role in the management of the program.

The staff has shown flexibility in adapting to the changing needs of the students, which is evident in their willingness to adopt new ESL and state standards and tests and to relocate to a new site, contributing to the overall success of the program. However, the students' own attitudes about INA and their smooth transition when they leave to enroll in the language centers are the most positive indicators of a fine program that is fulfilling its mission.

Learning to produce video programs in the school's media center is an integral part of language and content instruction at Newcomers High School in New York.

Conclusions and Future Directions

It is the first time in 30 years of experience working with English language learners that I see the light at the end of the tunnel. The gray areas are beginning to disappear and there seem to be definite solutions for effectively bringing newcomer English language learners into the school system by giving them specialized instruction and then making the transition into the larger programs in the home schools.

> —Dennis Terdy, Newcomer Center Director,
> Township High School District 214

The CREDE research project has vastly increased knowledge about secondary school newcomer programs for teachers, administrators, and policy makers. An increasing need in many districts across the country is to develop an understanding of effective ways to serve English language learners who are recent arrivals to the United States and who have no or low native language literacy, no English literacy, and interrupted schooling. ESL and bilingual programs have not always been able to meet the needs of these students, due in part to the fact that most of these programs are predicated on students having literacy skills. Without literacy, students have not had ready access to academic curricula and materials. Newcomer programs may prove critical to the success of these recent immigrant students because their academic needs are quickly assessed, and courses and curricula are designed to accelerate their learning. Newcomer programs may be particularly valuable to secondary school students who have less time than elementary school students in which to learn English and academic skills and to complete required course work before high school graduation.

This research project has presented the first national picture of newcomer programs for secondary school students as implemented in over 115 districts across 29 states and the District of Columbia. The database created as part of the study is unique, and the searchable, online version has been useful to practitioners and researchers around the world. By collating information about all of the identified programs, the project has provided an important resource for districts considering establishing a program, for newcomer sites interested in modifying their programs, for educators interested in visiting programs, for researchers interested in examining implementation practices and outcomes, and for policy makers interested in programmatic options for immigrant students.

One major characteristic of the newcomer programs studied was their attempt to serve students effectively by individualizing instruction to the greatest extent possible. Newcomer students come from a wide variety of educational, cultural, and linguistic backgrounds and thus require instruction tailored to meet their specific needs. Having knowledge of the students' personal circumstances and experiences influences decisions about curricula, instructional approaches, staffing, family services, and more. A second characteristic was the shared goal of socializing newcomer students and their parents to the schooling system in the United States, including school routines, classroom activity settings, and expectations for academic achievement.

As we learned more about secondary newcomer programs, we saw that they approached instruction from a cognitive development perspective. For example, although many students were at initial levels of literacy in either their native language or English when they entered a program, the curricula and instructional strategies were geared to the adolescent or young adult. Secondary school programs did not rely on primary-grade materials to teach literacy. If necessary, programs designed their own materials to fit their student population.

Newcomer programs were designed to begin instruction at the students' knowledge level, utilizing the native language as appropriate, then advance the students' learning with the assistance of more capable others—teachers, bilingual paraprofessionals, and peers. In this way, programs sought to prepare students for entry into the districts' regular language support programs or, in some cases, directly into regular or mainstream classrooms. Skillful teachers were careful to build on students' personal lives as the basis for many of their lessons. By linking the lessons to the students' experiences and life skills, teachers helped create access for these adolescent immigrant learners to the new subject matter and the new language.

Trends

During the course of the research study, we discovered several trends related to newcomer programs. First, there has been a growing awareness of this programmatic option for recent immigrants among educators of English language learners. When we began our study, we contacted state departments of education to identify newcomer programs in each state. Many told us that no such programs existed, but that turned out to be inaccurate. These states were unaware that this new model was being put into place at the local level. Because records for the newcomer students were not tagged any differently from those of other ESL or bilingual students when numbers were reported to the state, their distinct status was not apparent. Over time and through different dissemination activities, such as the online database, conferences, and articles, state departments of education and many others learned about newcomer programs and recognized those in their own regions. In fact, in 1999, the state of Illinois launched a newcomer initiative, encouraging local school districts to develop these programs as needed. The state offered technical assistance in the design phase and advice about funding.

The second trend we found was that an increasing number of newcomer programs were being established. Over 75% of the programs in our database began in the 1990s, while only 4% were established in the

1970s. This increase in programs in the 1990s reflects a shift in student demographics, with the arrival of more immigrant and refugee students fitting the definition of a newcomer (e.g., a student with no English and low native language literacy skills). Part of the increase could also be attributed to the growing awareness of this program model as an option for districts.

Third, more newcomer programs were being designed or modified to last for more than one school year. This trend is explained in part by the need to better prepare students for the rigorous, standards-based curricula that most school districts are enacting and for the high stakes accountability measures mandated by state and federal governments. Especially at the middle and high school levels, scores on tests become critical gatekeepers for grade promotion as well as graduation. Analyses of our data also suggest that the number of newcomer students who have large educational gaps and limited literacy and academic skills has increased in recent years. This increase has led newcomer programs to extend the allotted time that students spend in the program beyond the previously characteristic 1-year limit. As we saw with the INA newcomer program, one benefit of a longer stay is the potential for reducing the school dropout rate and keeping students on track toward a diploma or other career option.

A fourth trend was an increase in networking among programs. This was especially evident for districts in the exploration phase. Programs reported that the CREDE research study helped them identify existing sites to visit and showed them the range of program features that could be combined into a program model tailored for a specific group of newcomers. In addition, existing programs made connections across sites on their own, using the database profiles and project-sponsored listserv to solicit suggestions for literacy development strategies, assessment tools, student orientation materials, and more. As one program reported,

The newcomer study has significantly changed the district pro-
gram by providing insight into similar programs on the national
level. We have provided the administrators, principals, and school
board with vital information regarding the target group of stu-
dents. It has provided impetus for hiring more ESL-credentialed
personnel.

The final trend we noticed was an increase in formative program evaluations. More programs were assessing their program's implementation
to gather evidence of success (e.g., analyzing student test scores,
dropout rates, and attendance) and to identify areas for improvement.
This trend occurred in part because of the questions our study posed
regarding data on student progress and perhaps in larger part because
of increased pressure at district and state levels to justify a program's
existence, particularly in terms of funding. One program explained,
"The study has served as a self-evaluation and self-improvement tool. It
has helped us look more closely at each component of our program."

Coupled with an internal evaluation of the newcomer program's goals
was an increase in the broader view of how the program made an
impact on students after they left the program. Thus, more monitoring
of students who had made the transition into an ESL, bilingual, or mainstream program took place; consequently, more strategies to support
them in their new programs were put into practice.

Directions for Future Research

The CREDE study described here has made a significant contribution to our understanding of the range of newcomer programs in operation around the United States. Project staff have disseminated this information so newcomer sites can network with one another to share successful practices and develop strategies to overcome challenges. This study, however, is only the first step in a series of research studies that should be conducted on this programmatic alternative for immigrant English language learners.

There is a considerable need for research to evaluate newcomer programs' effectiveness compared to other language support programs available in a district. Interviews, classroom observations, and data collection and analysis across programs should be done to record instructional and assessment practices, attendance and dropout rates, and student achievement. Then staff can see how well former newcomer students do in the ESL or bilingual programs as compared with students who did not participate in the newcomer program. Policy makers and educators would like to know that newcomer programs make a difference and provide value for their cost. Preliminary data from some case study sites showed that newcomer students performed better than other English language learners on district assessments. This could be investigated more broadly.

Some evaluative comparisons of the different newcomer program models, within and across school districts, would be worthwhile so educators might determine, for instance, whether a separate-site, full-day bilingual program helps students make more or less academic progress than a full-day ESL program within a school. In particular, research could help identify the optimal program design for a given group of newcomer students and to achieve specific educational goals. Some program designs might be more effective for one group of learners than with another (e.g., Spanish speakers vs. speakers of other languages; those literate in their first language vs. those who are not). Given the large number of variables in design, these research studies need to be carefully planned in conjunction with the actual sites so that appropriate data will be collected, analyzed, and interpreted.

More research is needed on the most effective literacy strategies for adolescent learners, both for English language development and native language learning. Currently in the United States, mainstream educators are searching for approaches to reach native-English-speaking learners in middle and high school who do not read well. The newcomer students we describe in this book pose an even greater challenge as nonnative English speakers with limited formal schooling. Which methods help these students unlock the mystery of learning to read could be the subject of case studies and quasi-experimental research designs.

Another study might look at specific categories of newcomer students. For example, what effect does the entry of students at midterm have on the students who began the program on the first day of the school year? How do programs accommodate late-arriving students? Do more of these students remain longer in the program than those who began on the first day, and, if so, does extended time in the program lead to better success after exit? Researchers might also investigate the question of how best to serve older teenagers, many of whom are beyond the age of compulsory education and will pass the age of subsidized schooling before they acquire enough academic English and core credits to graduate from high school. What types of collaborations (e.g., with adult education programs, community colleges, GED programs, or vocational training schools) would provide appropriate educational paths for these students?

Assessment is another significant topic for future research, particularly in light of federal and state mandates. Newcomer staff are keenly interested in the best assessment practices for their students, who are most often unfamiliar with the culture and procedures of testing in U.S. schools, who lack the proficiency in English to read and understand the test questions, and who may lack the educational background in the subject areas being tested. A variety of research questions such as the following could be explored:

- What kind of testing accommodations might help newcomer students with low literacy skills participate in standardized testing?
- Under what conditions is it appropriate for newcomer students with interrupted formal education to take tests in certain content areas that they may never have studied, in a language they cannot yet read, write, or speak?
- What are some exemplary classroom-based assessment practices that can monitor newcomer student learning and guide subsequent instruction?

An additional research area is elementary newcomer programs. The CREDE study focused on middle school and high school settings, but we learned of a number of elementary programs as well. Similar research that documents and analyzes program models at the elementary school level would add to our growing understanding of this program alternative. One interesting research question, for example, might examine how literacy strategies for students in the upper elementary grades differ from those used with students in high school. Another question might investigate a sociocultural perspective to determine if the integration of newcomer students with the main student body in the school is accomplished more readily (and how) at the elementary level than at the secondary level.

Future Directions for Policy and Practice

The development and implementation of a newcomer program is an evolving process. Original design decisions may need modification once students begin their study. Additional materials may become available, the student population may shift, or new state and local education priorities may emerge; consequently, curricular emphases might change. What is important for the administrative and teaching staff of newcomer programs to build into their model is the flexibility to respond to these changes. Similarly, district policy makers must give programs a chance to mature and develop benchmarks for success along the way toward meeting their overall program goals.

In a related manner, all programs should have a formative evaluation process built into their design. Continual renewal and improvement can be accomplished when data are gathered through multiple means, such as test scores, grades, interviews, classroom observations, and curriculum reviews, and analyzed with the purpose of determining the effectiveness of the program model and staff. A summative evaluation should be conducted after a longer period of time, such as after 5 years of operation.

One strategy for accomplishing the evaluation plan is to institute a district policy to tag newcomer students in the assessment system so that while enrolled and after they exit the program their educational progress can continue to be tracked through data disaggregation. More districts are moving toward analyzing their student achievement data according to variables such as limited English proficient status as well as race and ethnicity. A newcomer designation in the system would provide a further distinction among English language learners. Such data analyses would not only help determine the relative value of the program but also help districts identify areas in need of additional resources to ensure student success in school.

Success for newcomer students rarely relies on implementing the grade-level curricula alone. Indeed, as we have shown through case studies and survey data, many programs create specialized courses for students in order to develop their literacy skills and close gaps in their educational background knowledge. What is needed are more courses like the *Fast Math* program developed in Fairfax County, Virginia. These courses would accelerate the curricula, covering material from more than one grade level in 1 year or less. *Fast Math,* as an example, can provide arithmetic instruction drawn from Grades 1–5 in one semester. Courses that integrate language and content learning objectives are particularly valuable for newcomer students. Appendix C includes a list of materials that have been designed specifically for newcomer students.

Success is also associated with classroom instructional practice. It should be district policy to hire only experienced and qualified teachers for the newcomer programs. Qualified means the teachers have had training in literacy development and sheltered instruction approaches. It means that they have knowledge of second language acquisition theory and cross-cultural awareness. It means they are certified in their area of instruction. And it means they know how to contextualize a lesson by incorporating the culture of the students or information about their home countries. Programs must maintain and enhance teaching quality by providing inservice opportunities directly connected to the teachers' work and the goals of the program.

Linked to the curricula and instruction are assessments. Newcomer programs may need to experiment to find the best measurement tools for their students. Certain English language assessments currently used for placement purposes might not be discrete enough to capture the differences among the lowest levels of proficiency. For instance, a student who is literate in his or her native language may score a zero on an English language assessment just as a nonliterate student might. The assessment therefore cannot distinguish who is literate and who is not, yet the educational agenda for these two types of students would be different from the outset of instruction. In addition, there is a need to develop new assessments that can measure academic English knowledge, knowledge connected to the content curricula and to the tasks students are required to perform in subject matter classes.

A final policy direction for districts implementing newcomer programs is establishing a better balance of other educational services. Fewer than half of the programs in our database participated in Title I, and fewer than 25% offered gifted and talented services to their students. Only slightly over half provided special education. The implementation of these kinds of services tends to occur as programs become more mature, but they should not be ignored at the outset. Identifying students for special education or gifted services is a challenge when students do not speak or read English, but assessments are being developed for these purposes and should be examined for use in any program.

Final Thoughts

Newcomer students, with limited literacy in any language and limited formal education, are particularly vulnerable in our school system and therefore deserve considerable attention. Newcomer programs offer an educational alternative that shows promise for developing students' competency in the language and literacy of instruction, pushing them toward greater cognitive complexity and promoting their academic success. These programs conform to local, state, and national goals for school reform. Through a newcomer program, students have better access to the educational system and better opportunities for future accomplishments.

The words from staff at the High School of World Cultures in New York City capture the sentiments of most educators involved in newcomer programs:

> We feel that through all that has been described in this paper [the 1999-2000 newcomer survey questionnaire], our students leave us feeling empowered as foreign students rather than victims of an anonymous system. Our students are helped to use what they know to find out what they need and where to go to get it. We are especially proud of the fact that we have been able to instill tolerance in students from dissenting countries as well as a sense of pride in appearance and the need to be a speaker, reader, and writer of English. Many people feel that students in a bilingual program don't learn English. We invite all to see our school in order to abandon this myth. We are proud of this school and all we have done. We know that to keep what we have means constant growth, change, and hard work.

References

Belluck, P. (1995, November 14). Complaint against newcomer school. *The New York Times,* p. B4.

Bush, T. (1992). International High School: Six years new. *College ESL, 2(1), 23-28.*

Chang, H. (1990). *Newcomer programs: Innovative efforts to meet the educational challenges of immigrant students.* San Francisco: California Tomorrow.

Cheng, L. (1999). *Challenges for Asian/Pacific American children and their teachers.* New York: ERIC Clearinghouse on Urban Education.

Coltrane, B. (2002). *English language learners and high-stakes tests: An overview of the issues.* Washington, DC: ERIC Clearinghouse on Languages and Linguistics.

Constantino, R., & Lavadenz, M. (1993). Newcomer schools: First impressions. *Peabody Journal of Education, 69*(1), 82-101.

Cummins, J. (1981). The role of primary language development in promoting education success for language minority students. In *Schooling and language minority students: A theoretical framework* (pp. 3-49). Los Angeles: California State University; Evaluation, Dissemination and Assessment Center.

Doherty, K. M., & Skinner, R. A. (2003). State of the states. *Education Week, 22*(17), 75-78, 88.

Dufresne, J., & Hall, S. (1997). LEAP English Academy: An alternative high school for newcomers to the United States. *MINNE-WI TESOL Journal, 14,* 1-17.

Echevarria, J., Vogt, M. E., & Short, D. J. (2004). *Making content comprehensible for English learners: The SIOP model* (2nd ed.). Newton, MA: Allyn & Bacon.

Friedlander, M. (1991). *The newcomer program: Helping immigrant students succeed in U.S. schools* (Program Information Guide No. 8). Washington, DC: National Clearinghouse for Bilingual Education. Retrieved November 14, 2003, from www.ncela.gwu.edu/ncbepubs/pigs/pig8.htm

Gonzalez, R. (1994). *Title VII newcomer program: Final report 1993-1994.* Austin, TX: Austin Independent School District, Office of Research and Evaluation.

Hamayan, E. (1994). Language development of low-literacy students. In F. Genesee (Ed.), *Educating second language children* (pp. 278-300). New York: Cambridge University Press.

Helman, M., & Buchanan, K. (1993). *Reforming mathematics instruction for ESL literacy students* (Program Information Guide No. 15). Washington, DC: National Clearinghouse for Bilingual Education. Retrieved November 14, 2003, from www.ncela.gwu.edu/ncbepubs/pigs/pig15.htm

Jamieson, A., Curry, A., & Martinez, G. (2001). School enrollment in the United States—Social and economic characteristics of students. *Current Population Reports* (P20-533). Washington, DC: U.S. Government Printing Office.

Latinos in education: Early childhood, elementary, undergraduate, graduate. (1999). Washington, DC: White House Initiative on Educational Excellence for Hispanic Americans. (ERIC Document Reproduction Service No. ED440817)

Mace-Matluck, B., Alexander-Kasparik, R., & Queen, R. (1998). *Through the golden door: Effective educational approaches for immigrant adolescents with limited schooling.* Washington, DC, and McHenry, IL: Center for Applied Linguistics and Delta Systems.

McDonnell, L., & Hill, P. (1993). *Newcomers in American schools: Meeting the educational needs of immigrant youth.* Santa Monica, CA: RAND.

Menken, K. (2000). *What are the critical issues in wide-scale assessment of English language learners?* (Issue Brief No. 6). Washington, DC: National Clearinghouse for Bilingual Education.

Moran, C., Stobbe, J., Tinajero, A., & Tinajero, J. V. (1993). Strategies for working with overage students. In J. V. Tinajero & A. F. Ada (Eds.), *The power of two languages: Literacy and biliteracy for Spanish-speaking students* (pp. 117-131). New York: Macmillan/McGraw- Hill.

National Clearinghouse for English Language Acquisition. (2002). *The growing numbers of limited English proficient students.* Retrieved December 1, 2002, from www.ncela.gwu.edu/states/stateposter.pdf

New York State Education Department, Office of Bilingual Education, & Nassau BOCES Bilingual/ESL Technical Assistance Center. (1997). *Proceedings of the New York State symposium on the education of overage limited English proficient students with interrupted formal schooling.* Albany: University of the State of New York, New York State Education Department.

Olsen, L. (2000, Autumn). Learning English and learning America: Immigrants in the center of a storm. *Theory into Practice, 39*(4), 196-202.

Olsen, L., & Dowell, C. (1989). *Bridges: Promising programs for the education of immigrant children.* San Francisco: California Tomorrow.

Olsen, L., Jaramillo, A., McCall-Perez, Z., & White, J. (1999). *Igniting change for immigrant students: Portraits of three high schools.* Oakland: California Tomorrow.

Pilon, B. (1993). Newcomers find hope and caring in unique LAUSD high school. *CASP Today, 42*(3),

Ruiz-de-Velasco, J., & Fix, M. (2000). *Overlooked and underserved: Immigrant students in U.S. secondary schools.* Washington, DC: Urban Institute.

Schnur, B. (1999, April). A newcomer's high school. *Educational Leadership, 56*(7), 50-52.

Short, D., & Boyson, B. (2000). *Directory of secondary newcomer programs in the U.S.: Revised 2000.* Washington, DC: Center for Research on Education, Diversity & Excellence; and Center for Applied Linguistics.

Te, B. (1997). *Unfamiliar partners: Asian parents and United States public schools.* Boston: National Coalition of Advocates for Students.

Thomas, W. P., & Collier, V. P. (2002). *A national study of school effectiveness for language minority students' long-term academic achievement.* Santa Cruz, CA: Center for Research on Education, Diversity & Excellence.

Waggoner, D. (1999). Who are secondary newcomer and linguistically different youth? In C. Faltis & P. Wolfe (Eds.), *So much to say: Adolescents, bilingualism, and ESL in secondary schools* (pp. 13-41). New York: Teachers College Press.

Appendix A

Key Features of
Secondary Newcomer Programs

The matrix on the following pages identifies the 115 programs included in this study, their locations, and key features at a glance. The programs are organized by state. Within each state, the programs are listed alphabetically in the following order: middle school, high school, and middle/high school combination. The following key features of the programs are highlighted in this matrix: school level, type of community setting, type of site, length of daily program, length of enrollment in the program, and type of instruction offered.

Key Features of Secondary Newcomer Programs
2000

Legend: ● = filled, ○ = open circle

	School Level: Middle school	High school	Middle and high school combined	Type of Community: Urban/metropolitan	Suburban	Rural	Program Location: Separate site or whole school	Program within a school [1]	Length of Daily Program: Full day	Half day or less	After school	Length of Enrollment in Program: Less than one school year	One school year	More than one school year [2]	Instruction: Cross-cultural/Orientation to U.S.	Sheltered content instruction	Content in native language(s)
Alaska																	
Anchorage School District	○	○	●	●	○	○	●	○	○	●	○	○	●	○	●	●	○
California																	
Hyde Junior High School	●	○	○	○	○	●	○	●	○	●	○	○	○	●	●	●	○
Matthew Gage Middle School	●	○	○	○	●	○	○	●	●	○	○	○	○	●	○	●	●
Sunnyvale School District	●	○	○	●	○	○	○	●	○	●	○	○	○	●	●	●	○
Alhambra School District	○	●	○	○	●	○	○	●	●	○	○	○	●	○	●	●	○
Belmont High School	○	●	○	●	○	○	○	●	●	○	○	●	○	○	●	●	●
Crawford High School	○	●	○	●	○	○	○	●	●	●	○	○	○	●	●	●	●
El Modena High School	○	●	○	○	●	○	○	●	●	○	○	●	○	○	●	●	●
Escondido Union High School District	○	●	○	○	●	○	●	○	●	○	○	○	○	●	●	●	●
Herbert Hoover High School	○	●	○	●	○	○	○	●	●	○	○	●	○	○	●	●	●
Laguna Hills High School	○	●	○	○	●	○	○	●	●	○	○	●	○	○	●	●	●
Newcomer High School	○	●	○	●	○	○	●	○	●	○	○	○	●	○	●	●	●
Polytechnic High School	○	●	○	●	○	○	○	●	●	○	○	○	○	●	●	●	●
Sequoia High School	○	●	○	●	○	○	○	●	●	○	○	○	○	●	○	●	○
Calexico Unified School District	○	○	●	○	○	●	○	●	○	○	●	○	○	●	●	●	○
Hayward High School	○	○	●	●	○	○	○	●	●	○	○	○	○	●	●	●	●
Colorado																	
Newcomer Pathways - High School	○	●	○	●	○	○	○	●	●	●	○	●	○	○	●	●	●
Connecticut																	
John Winthrop Middle School	●	○	○	●	○	○	○	●	●	○	○	○	○	●	●	●	●

Key Features of Secondary Newcomer Programs
2000

Column categories (with indicators marked by filled ● and open ○ circles):

- **School Level:** Middle school; High school; Middle and high school combined
- **Type of Community:** Urban/metropolitan; Suburban; Rural
- **Program Location:** Separate site or whole school; Program within a school
- **Length of Daily Program [1]:** Full day or less; Half day or less; After school
- **Length of Enrollment in Program:** Less than one school year; One school year; More than one school year
- **Instruction:** Cross-cultural/Orientation to U.S.; Sheltered content instruction [2]; Content in native language(s)

Programs listed:

Bassick High School

District of Columbia
Bell Multicultural High School

Florida
Miami-Dade County Public Schools

Georgia
DeKalb County School System, ESOL Lab
DeKalb County School System, Intake/ISC

Illinois
César E. Chávez Multicultural Academic Center
Newcomers' Interim Service Center
César E. Chávez Junior Academy
Taft High School

Iowa
Sioux City Community Schools - Middle
Des Moines - Central Campus
Sioux City Community Schools - High

Kansas
East High School
North High School
Garden City Intake Center

Key Features of Secondary Newcomer Programs

2000

Column headings (left to right):

School Level — Middle school · High school · Middle and high school combined

Type of Community — Urban/metropolitan · Suburban · Rural

Program Location — Separate site or whole school · Program within a school

Length of Daily Program — Full day · Half day or less · After school

Length of Enrollment in Program — Less than one school year · One school year · More than one school year

Instruction — Cross-cultural/Orientation to U.S. · Sheltered content instruction [1] · Content in native language(s) [2]

Maryland
- Julius West Middle School
- Montgomery County Public Schools
- Prince George's County Public Schools

Massachusetts
- Williams South Middle School
- Chelsea High School

Michigan
- Berkley Public Schools
- Pathfinders Alternative Middle/High School

Minnesota
- John Adams Middle School, ISD 535
- Abraham Lincoln High School
- Century High School
- Saint Paul Public Schools

Missouri
- Northeast Middle School
- Northeast High School

Nebraska
- South Sioux City Community Schools

Key Features of Secondary Newcomer Programs 2000

Column categories (top, rotated):

- **Instruction:** Sheltered content instruction / Cross-cultural/Orientation to U.S. / Content in native language(s)
- **Length of Enrollment in Program:** One school year / Less than one school year / More than one school year
- **Length of Daily Program:** Full day / Half day or less / After school
- **Program Location:** Separate site or whole school / Program within a school
- **Type of Community:** Urban/metropolitan / Suburban / Rural
- **School Level:** Middle school / High school / Middle and high school combined

Nevada
- Clark County School District
- Washoe County School District

New Jersey
- Costley Middle School
- Jersey City School District
- Paterson Public Schools, Port-of-Entry
- Perth Amboy Public Schools - Middle
- Abraham Clark High School
- Dover High School
- East Orange High School
- Memorial High School
- Paterson Public Schools, ACES Program
- Perth Amboy Public Schools - High
- Union Hill High School
- Passaic Learning Center

New Mexico
- Mayfield High School

New York
- Intermediate School 235
- Inwood Intermediate School 52
- Jackie Robinson Intermediate School 320

Key Features of Secondary Newcomer Programs
2000

School	School Level		Type of Community			Program Location		Length of Daily Program			Length of Enrollment in Program		Instruction		
	Middle school	High school	Middle and high school combined	Urban/metropolitan	Suburban	Rural	Program within a school	Separate site or whole school	After school	Half day or less	Full day	Less than one school year	One school year	More than one school year	Cross-cultural/Orientation to U.S.	Sheltered content instruction	Content in native language(s)
John J. Pershing Intermediate School 220	•			•			○			•		○		•	•	•	•
Somers Intermediate School 252	•			•			•			•		○		○	•	•	○
Brooklyn International High School, The		•		•			○			○		•		○	•	•	○
Gregorio Luperon Preparatory School		•		•			○			•		•		○	○	•	•
High School of World Cultures		•		•			○			•		•		○	•	•	•
International High School, The		•		•			•			•		•		○	•	•	•
John Bowne High School		•		•			○			•		•		○	•	•	•
Liberty High School		•		•			○			•		•		○	•	•	•
Manhattan International High School, The		•		•			○			•		•		○	•	•	○
Nassau Tech		•			•		•			•		○		○	•	•	○
Newcomers High School, The		•		•			○			•		•		○	•	•	○
Theodore Roosevelt High School		•		•			○			•		•		○			
North Carolina																	
Independence High School		○		•			•			•		○		○	○	•	○
Olympic High School		○		•			•			•		○		•	○	•	○
West Charlotte High School		○		•			•			•		○		○	○	•	○
Burlington School District		•			○		○			•		•		•	•	•	•
Ohio																	
Columbus Public Schools		○		•			•			•		○		•	○	○	○
Oklahoma																	
Capitol Hill High School		○		•			○			•		•		○	•	•	○

Key Features of Secondary Newcomer Programs
2000

Column categories (left to right):

Instruction
- Content in native language(s)
- Sheltered content instruction
- Cross-cultural/Orientation to U.S. [2]

Length of Enrollment in Program
- More than one school year
- One school year
- Less than one school year

Length of Daily Program
- After school
- Half day or less
- Full day [1]

Program Location
- Program within a school
- Separate site or whole school

Type of Community
- Rural
- Suburban
- Urban/metropolitan

School Level
- Middle and high school combined
- High school
- Middle school

Oregon
- Hermiston High School
- Reynolds School District
- Woodburn Public Schools

Pennsylvania
- South Philadelphia High School
- State College High School - South

Texas
- Barbara Bush Middle School
- Coppell Middle School-West
- Corpus Christi Independent School District
- Jane Long Middle School
- Alief Independent School District
- Bowie High School
- Coppell High School
- John H. Reagan High School
- L. G. Pinkston High School
- Lanier High School
- Newman Smith High School
- North Dallas High School
- Travis High School
- Aldine Independent School District

Key Features of Secondary Newcomer Programs
2000

	School Level			Type of Community			Program Location		Length of Daily Program			Length of Enrollment in Program			Instruction		
	Middle school	High school	Middle and high school combined	Urban/metropolitan	Suburban	Rural	Separate site or whole school	Program within a school [1]	Full day	Half day or less	After school	Less than one school year	One school year	More than one school year [2]	Cross-cultural/Orientation to U.S.	Sheltered content instruction	Content in native language(s)
International Newcomer Academy	○	○	●	●	○	○	●	○	●	○	○	○	●	○	●	●	●
Irving Independent School District	○	○	●	○	●	○	●	○	●	○	○	○	○	●	●	●	●
Workman Junior High School	○	○	●	●	○	○	○	●	●	○	○	○	○	●	●	●	○
Utah																	
ELD Program, Family Center	○	●	○	●	○	○	●	○	●	○	○	○	●	○	●	●	●
Virginia																	
Fairfax County Public Schools	○	●	○	○	●	○	○	●	●	○	○	○	○	●	○	●	●
Washington																	
Pioneer Middle School	●	○	○	○	○	●	○	●	○	●	○	○	●	○	●	●	●
Washington Middle School	●	○	○	●	○	○	○	●	●	○	○	○	○	●	●	●	●
A. C. Davis High School	○	●	○	●	○	○	○	●	●	●	○	○	●	○	●	●	●
Wenatchee High School	○	●	○	○	○	●	○	●	○	●	○	○	●	○	●	●	●
Highline School District	○	○	●	●	○	○	○	●	●	○	○	○	○	●	●	●	○
Seattle School District	○	○	●	●	○	○	●	○	●	○	○	○	○	●	●	●	○
Wisconsin																	
Green Bay Area Public Schools	○	○	●	●	○	○	○	●	●	○	○	○	○	●	●	●	●
Wausau School District	○	○	●	○	○	●	○	●	○	●	●	○	○	●	●	●	○

[1] The matrix category, *Program within a school,* refers to programs that are part of a fuller set of programs within one school. It includes programs that serve only the students who attend the school where the program is located and programs that serve students from more than one home school, including the one where it is located.

[2] The matrix category, *More than 1 school year,* includes programs that are designated as 1 school year but also offer a summer program as well as programs that are designated as more than 1 school year (e.g., three- or four-semester programs).

Appendix B

Contact Information for Case Study Sites

Newcomer Program
César Chávez Multicultural Academic Center
Mr. Pedro Beiza, Program Coordinator
4747 S. Marshfield Avenue
Chicago, IL 60609
Phone: (773) 535-4641

Liberty High School
Ms. Melodee Khristan, Principal
250 W. 18th Street
New York, NY 10011
Phone: (212) 691-C668

International Newcomer Academy
Mr. Carlos Ayala, Principal
7000 Camp Bowie
Fort Worth, TX 76116
Phone: (817) 570-5900

Appendix C

Resources from Programs

School's Cool: An Orientation to U.S. Schools
Judy Bakenhus and Trude Skolnick
Produced by Emergency Immigrant Education Program, Los Angeles
Unified School District, Language Acquisition Branch
Bellagio Road Newcomer Center
11301 Bellagio Road, Room 3
Los Angeles, CA 90040
Phone: (310) 471-1303
Fax: (310) 472-1981

An Orientation to Life in the United States: A Curriculum to Help Immigrant Latino Adolescents and Their Parents Adjust
Beth Hood
Next Step Charter School
1419 Columbia Road, NW
Washington, DC 20009
Phone: (202) 319-2245

FAST Math
Jane E. LeRoy
The FAST Math curriculum is available from:
National Clearinghouse on English Language Acquisition and Language
Instructional Programs
Phone: 1-800-321-6223 or 202-467-0867

Related resources:
Reforming Mathematics Instruction for ESL Literacy Students
www.ncela.gwu.edu/ncbepubs/pigs/pig15.htm

Fairfax County Public Schools FAST Math page:
www.fcps.edu/dis/OESOL/fastmath.htm

About the Authors

Deborah J. Short, Ph. D., directs the Language Education and Academic Development division at the Center for Applied Linguistics (CAL) in Washington, DC. She has worked as a teacher, staff developer, researcher, and curriculum/materials developer in language minority education for more than 20 years. She investigates program designs for English language learners, including newcomer programs. She also co-developed and conducts school-based research on the SIOP Model and directed the national PreK–12 ESL Standards and Assessment project for TESOL.

Beverly Boyson has been a researcher at the Center for Applied Linguistics since 1997 with projects related to newcomer programs for secondary students and the development of the Sheltered Instruction Observation Protocol (SIOP) Model for integrating content and language instruction in K-12 classrooms. She conducts staff development workshops on the SIOP Model for school districts across the country. She has also worked at CAL in the development of foreign language assessments and conducts training workshops on the administration of oral proficiency assessments for elementary and middle school students.

PROFESSIONAL DEVELOPMENT: NEWCOMER AND IMMIGRANT EDUCATION

Students from non-English-speaking backgrounds are the fastest growing segment of the K-12 student population in the United States. An increasing number of these students are newcomers—recent arrivals to the United States who have very limited or no English language proficiency and who often have had limited formal education in their native countries.

CAL provides a number of resources designed to support the implementation of a relatively new model for serving these language minority students—the newcomer program.

For more information about CAL's products and services for newcomers, email CAL at info@cal.org or call 202-362-0700.

Secondary School Newcomer Programs in the United States

Beverly A. Boyson & Deborah J. Short

This data-rich report presents a 4-year study of newcomer programs in the United States. Researchers used a detailed questionnaire to collect and synthesize data on many characteristics of existing newcomer programs, describing the populations served and the rationale for recent program development. The report also presents findings regarding program features, instructional design, student assessment, staffing, professional development, and parent and community connections.

$8.00   2003   CREDE-9088RR12   33 pp.

Proceedings of the First National Conference for Educators of Newcomer Students

Beverly A. Boyson, Bronwyn Coltrane, & Deborah J. Short (Editors)

These proceedings offer summaries of more than 35 presentations from this 2002 conference that focused on design, curriculum and instruction, and professional development in elementary and secondary newcomer programs.

$18.50   2003   CREDE-9088NCP   66 pp.

Directory of Secondary Newcomer Programs in the United States

Deborah J. Short & Beverly A. Boyson

This directory contains profiles of 115 middle and high school newcomer programs across 196 sites in 29 states and the District of Columbia. These programs serve recent immigrant secondary school students with little or no English proficiency and often limited formal schooling.

$35.00   2000   CREDE-9088DSN   542 pp.

Topics In Immigrant Education Series
Center for Applied Linguistics & Delta Systems Co., Inc.

Into, Through, and Beyond Secondary School: Critical Transitions for Immigrant Youths
Tamara Lucas

This book presents four principles on which to base a successful approach to this issue, then describes and provides contact information for United States schools, programs, and organizations that are successfully implementing these strategies.
$20.95   1997   DEL-1-887744-03-7   294 pp.

Through the Golden Door: Educational Approaches for Immigrant Adolescents with Limited Schooling
Betty J. Mace-Matluck, Rosalind Alexander-Kaparik, & Robin M. Queen

This book provides guidelines for school administrators and teachers, profiles four programs designed to serve these students, identifies features of successful programs, and provides program contacts and resources.
$20.95   1999   DEL-1-887744-07-X   152 pp.

Access and Engagement: Program Design and Instructional Approaches for Immigrant Students in Secondary School
Aída Walqui

This book provides in-depth profiles of six immigrant high school students with diverse backgrounds, describes four programs in the U.S., and identifies 10 characteristics of schools and programs that foster effective teaching for immigrant youth.
$20.95   2000   DEL-1-887744-09-6   240 pp.

New Concepts for New Challenges: Professional Development for Teachers of Immigrant Youth
Josué M. González & Linda Darling-Hammond

This book is a valuable resource to help school staff prepare for dealing with immigrant students. The authors describe promising new structures and practices for professional development and profile several highly successful preservice and insevice programs.
$20.95   1997   DEL-1-887744-04-5   168 pp.

It's easy to order publications and resources from the CAL*store*

Click:	Call:	Fax:
calstore@cal.org	**1-800-551-3709**	**1-888-700-3629**
	M-F 9am-5pm EST	

Professional Practice Series

Jeanne Rennie and Joy Kreeft Peyton, Series Editors

Teachers and administrators need ready access to clear and reliable information about effective practices in language education. The *Professional Practice Series*, published by the Center for Applied Linguistics and Delta Systems, is designed to provide practitioners with accessible, timely information, supported by theory and research, on topics, trends, and techniques in language teaching. The following volumes in the series are now available:

English Language Learners with Special Education Needs: Identification, Assessment, and Instruction

Alfredo J. Artiles & Alba A. Ortiz, Editors

This book describes the challenges involved in identifying, placing, and teaching English language learners with special education needs. It describes model programs and approaches, including early intervention programs, assessment methods, parent/school collaboration, and native and dual language instruction. All students deserve a quality education that meets their individual needs and capitalizes on their strengths. This book is designed to help achieve that goal.

$20.53   2002   DEL-887744-69-X   250 pp.

Lessons Learned: Model Early Foreign Language Programs

by Douglas F. Gilzow & Lucinda E. Branaman

This book describes seven successful foreign language programs for students in Grades K–8 in Connecticut, Florida, Maryland, Massachusetts, North Carolina, Ohio, and Oregon. Each chapter focuses on a particular program, describing the strategies and techniques used by effective teachers and administrators and offering practical guidelines and suggestions to help others implement similar strategies in their own classrooms, schools, and districts.

$19.95   2000   DEL-1-887744-63-0   217 pp.

Language by Video: An Overview of Foreign Language Instructional Videos for Children

Nancy C. Rhodes & Ingrid Pufahl

Language by Video describes how foreign language instructional videos are used in a variety of settings as a supplement or alternative to traditional foreign language instruction for elementary school students. The information is presented in a user-friendly format, with practical implications and recommendations as well as suggestions for future research on this topic. This book will be of special interest to schools and educators considering alternatives to traditional foreign language instruction.

$20.95   2004   DEL-1-887744-89-4